NATIONAL TRUST

Book of Jam

NATIONAL TRUST

Book of Jam

Sara Lewis

National Trust

Published by National Trust Books
An imprint of HarperCollins Publishers
1 London Bridge Street
London SE1 9GF
www.harpercollins.co.uk

HarperCollins Publishers
1st Floor, Watermarque Building, Ringsend Road, Dublin 4, Ireland

First published in 2019

ISBN: 9781911358602

10 9 8 7 6 5 4 3 2

Printed and bound in Latvia

If you would like to comment on any aspect of this book, please contact us
at the above address or national.trust@harpercollins.co.uk

National Trust publications are available at National Trust shops or online at
nationaltrustbooks.co.uk

Contents

Introduction

Jam making is a kind of alchemy, in which fresh fruit is miraculously transformed and given a long and happy life. The magic is revealed when you open a jar of strawberry jam and the wonderful fragrance takes you right back to a warm summer day, a glistening spoonful of blackberry jam conjures up memories of autumn walks.

Jam making is no longer an essential part of domestic economy. In the past, both individual households and the grand houses now cared for by the National Trust regularly set aside time to preserve produce when it was in season. Yet even if we don't spend quite as much time in the kitchen as our mothers or grandmothers did, there is something deeply satisfying about making a batch of jam.

It's hard to imagine that sugar was once so expensive that only the very rich could enjoy jam – not in the form we enjoy it today but served on small silver spoons to end a grand meal. While preserves may have been served as spoon treats at the opulent court of Louis XIV at Versailles or Elizabethan banquets, the Romans and Greeks were perhaps the first to cook quinces, figs, cherries and other seasonal fruits with honey to make a smooth thick preserve.

If you are new to jam making, this book begins with a few basics to help you on your way. If you are an old hand, you will find new and unusual fruit combinations to inspire you. Jam-packed with recipes, it includes timeless favourites and extra-fruity reduced-sugar jams, crystal clear fruit jellies and firm, sliceable fruit cheeses, buttery fruit curds and Britain's favourite breakfast spread, marmalade.

The basics

Jams, fruit jellies and marmalades all demonstrate a delicate balance of fruit, sugar, acidity and pectin. Sugar contributes to the sweetness of the jam while also acting as a preservative for long-term storage. When heated, the pectin naturally found in the fruit seeds, pips, cores and skins is released and together with the right balance of acidity from the fruits, natural fruit acids form a gel to make a spreadable and intensely fruity preserve. Many recipes suggest mixing soft fruits with sugar and leaving to macerate so that the sugar draws out the water before cooking to reduce cooking time. This is so that soft fruits, such as strawberries and cherries, don't lose too much colour during cooking. For firmer fruits, such as gooseberries, currants or citrus fruit, cook in a little water to soften before boiling with sugar, as once the sugar is added the skins will not soften further. Some fruits naturally contain more pectin than others – boost the set by adding extra fresh lemon juice, or use jam sugar with added pectin and citric acid, or try with a mix of high- and low-pectin fruits.

Equipment

Traditionally jams are cooked in a preserving pan – a large pan with sloping sides to aid evaporation and a thick heavy base to help prevent the mixture burning and sticking as it boils. Preserving pans vary in size but are generally about 30cm across the top and about 18cm deep. A stainless steel preserving pan will last a lifetime. Shop around as prices vary and if you are not sure how often you will make jam you may be able to pick up a pre-loved bargain from eBay (check the size as some of the older ones are enormous) or substitute a large heavy-based stock pot or pasta pan. If you have an induction hob, check that your preserving pan is suitable.

The most crucial thing is that there is enough room in the pan for the jam to boil up as it comes to setting point. Once the fruit and sugar are in the pan it should be just under half full; any fuller and it could boil over. However, if you are making only a small quantity of jam, a large preserving pan may be too big; if the jam is too thinly spread over the base of the pan, it will be more likely to stick and burn. You will need a long-handled wooden spoon for stirring, and a slotted spoon – the kind with small holes that you might use to scoop peas out of a pan of water – for skimming off any scum. You will also need kitchen scales, a chopping board and a good sharp knife, a lemon squeezer, vegetable peeler and a couple of saucers to use when testing for set – chill them in the fridge before you begin making the jam. A food processor with a metal blade, a thin slicing blade and citrus squeezer will save you lots of preparation time.

When using citrus fruits, especially in marmalade making, you will need to tie the pips and squeezed citrus shells in a 'bag' made from muslin or a linen tea towel, cut into squares, and some fine string.

If you hope to make jam frequently, it is worth investing in a sugar thermometer so you can see when the jam is getting near to setting point. A metal jam funnel helps to avoid sticky spillages as you ladle the jam into the warm jars. For jelly fans, you will need a jelly bag, ideally with a stand, for the cooked fruit to drip through.

Top of the pots
While good cookshops sell jam jars, it's more satisfying to re-use your old jars. Assorted sizes are fine, but if the last jar isn't full to the brim store it in the fridge and use within a few weeks. Soak them in warm water so that you can remove the labels, then wash jars and lids thoroughly in hot soapy water, rinse and dry. Keep in a cupboard or inside your preserving pan so that they are ready and waiting.

Sterilise them in a warm oven just before filling. Stand the clean jars and their lids separately in a roasting tin and place in a preheated oven set to 130°C (or in a low Aga oven) for 15 minutes; don't worry if you get delayed and the jars are in the oven for a little longer.

Choosing fruit
While it can be tempting to use up softer overripe fruit in jam, it is best not to, as ripe fruit begins to lose its pectin. Slightly underripe or just-ripe fruit has the most flavour and maximum amounts of pectin.

Which sugar to use

Jam sugar with added pectin and citric acid is used for many jams and jellies to ensure the set of low-pectin fruits such as strawberries, cherries, apricots and peaches. Preserving sugar is most suitable for fruits with a higher pectin level, such as gooseberries, cooking apples, quinces, black and red currants, and damsons. Both these sugars have larger crystals than granulated sugar and produce slightly less scum, which is particularly important when making jellies.

Granulated sugar, with its smaller crystals, is ideal for marmalade, fruit cheeses, butters and curds; it can also be used in place of preserving sugar if you run out. For toffee-like flavours in some jams or marmalades, it is nice to substitute some of the white sugar for light or dark muscovado sugar or honey.

Back in the days when homes were colder and larders often a little damp, warming the sugar was recommended. Nowadays this is not critical unless making a large amount of jam at a time. Whichever sugar you use, it must be completely dissolved before bringing the jam or jelly to the boil to prevent crystals forming in the finished jam.

Simmer, boil and skim

The first stage in jam making is to simmer the fruit until it softens; this releases the pectin. Next add sugar and cook gently until the sugar has completely dissolved. Now it's time to bring the mixture quickly to boiling point and boil rapidly until setting point is reached; this will depend on the type of fruit and the amounts of pectin. You can tell when a jam is almost ready, as the fast rolling boil will change to a slower, more relaxed boil. The tiny air bubbles will disappear and the mixture will look glossy and feel thicker as you stir.

The movement of the boiling mixture pushes scum to the outer edges of the pan, where it is easier to skim off. Leaving the scum in can lead to unattractive white lumps in your jam. However don't skim too often or you will lose too much jam. Adding a small knob of butter after setting point is reached breaks the surface tension and magically disperses any remaining scum.

How to test for setting point

1 Temperature test Once the sugar has dissolved, add a sugar thermometer and bring the mixture to boiling point, then boil rapidly for 5–15 minutes for jams and jellies or 15–20 minutes for marmalade. The jam is ready when it reaches 105°C, although jams made with very high-pectin fruits or with jam sugar may set a degree or two below that. For best results do the saucer test to confirm the set.

2 Flake test As you stir the jam as it boils, lift the wooden spoon out of the pan and turn it on its side, then watch as the jam falls from the spoon. As the jam begins to thicken it will change from a thin stream to a thicker tear-shaped drop that is held by the rim of the spoon for a few seconds. At this point turn off the heat so that the jam doesn't overboil and darken, and move on to the saucer test.

3 Saucer test Take the pan off the heat, spoon a little of the jam on to a chilled saucer and put into the fridge for 5 minutes. When you push your finger through the cooled jam it should wrinkle and leave a trail so that you can see the saucer. If the jam runs back into a pool then it is not ready; put the pan back on the heat and boil for a few more minutes, and then turn off the heat again and retest.

When the jam is ready, ladle it into the sterilised jars while it is still hot. Adding hot jam to warmed jars also means there is less likelihood of them cracking. If the jam has large pieces of fruit, leave it to stand for 10–15 minutes before adding to the jars; it will thicken slightly and the pieces of fruit won't rise to the top of the jar. If you have a sugar thermometer the jam should be potted before it drops to 85°C.

Traditionally jams are covered with a waxed disc and cellophane top secured with an elastic band. If using these, it is important that the waxed disc is the right size: it should fit the inside of the jar perfectly and should be lightly pressed onto the surface of the hot jam so that the heat melts the waxed layer and makes a seal. The cellophane top is really a dust cover. Screw-topped lids are much more convenient once the jar has been opened. If using screw tops, make sure to fill the jar of jam right to the brim, and then screw on the lid immediately. As the preserve cools it will shrink and form a vacuum. If you add a waxed disc this will interfere with the vacuum. Don't forget to label and date the filled jars; it is amazing how quickly you will forget what is inside.

Storage

If sealed well, most jams, jellies, marmalades and fruit cheeses will keep for up to a year in a cool dark place, some even longer. Once opened the jar should be kept in the fridge and the contents eaten within a few weeks. Conserves and fruit butters are best eaten within 6 months as they contain slightly less sugar than traditional jams. Reduced-sugar jams are best stored in the fridge and used within a month. Fruit curds made with butter and eggs should also be stored in the fridge and eaten within 2 weeks.

Conserves

Jam as we know it emerged in the late nineteenth century with a recognised ratio of 1:1 fruit to sugar. Sugar is not only needed to add sweetness to tangy fruits but is also important as a preservative. With changing tastes many people are trying to cut down on the amount of sugar they consume. Conserves generally have a higher proportion of fruit to sugar, which makes for a slightly softer set preserve. All jams are conserves, but not all conserves are jams. In the UK, jam must contain 60% sugar, which includes naturally occurring fruit sugars; if less, it must be labelled a reduced-sugar jam or conserve. Fruit preserves with less than 50% sugar are termed fruit spreads.

Notes

Read the recipe through before starting, to ensure you have all the equipment you need. Note that some recipes need to be left for several hours or overnight before cooking the preserve.

All spoon measurements are level.
1 teaspoon = 5ml
1 tablespoon = 15ml
Use medium eggs

Jams

Raspberry and rhubarb jam

Rhubarb ranges in colour from the pretty pink early forced stems of spring through to the larger deeper pink and green-tinged stems of summer. Adding raspberries to rhubarb helps to boost the colour of the finished jam, while making a few raspberries go further. Try this jam spread over sponge cakes in the base of a trifle or to sandwich a Victoria sponge.

1kg trimmed rhubarb, thickly sliced
400g raspberries
4 tbsp water
1.4kg preserving sugar
Juice of 2 lemons
15g unsalted butter (optional)

Add the rhubarb, raspberries and water to a preserving pan, cover and cook over a low heat for 10 minutes, stirring from time to time, until the fruit has softened and the juices have begun to run.

Pour in the sugar and lemon juice, stir together and continue to cook over a low heat, stirring from time to time, until the sugar has completely dissolved. Bring to the boil and boil rapidly for 10–15 minutes, stirring from time to time, until setting point is reached.

Skim off any scum then take off the heat and stir in the butter to disperse any remaining scum, if needed. Ladle the hot jam into warmed sterilised jars right to the top, then screw on lids or cover with waxed discs and cellophane tops secured with elastic bands. Leave to cool, then label and date. Store in a cool place.

Apricot and vanilla jam

Popular in France, this exquisite combination of fresh apricots and tiny pieces of vanilla is a gourmet delight. Perfect served with a warm croissant for a relaxed Sunday breakfast.

1kg apricots, quartered and stoned
Juice of 1 lemon
6 tbsp water

1 vanilla pod
1kg jam sugar with added pectin
15g unsalted butter (optional)

Add the apricots, lemon juice and water to a preserving pan. Slit the vanilla pod lengthways, scrape out the soft black seeds and add to the apricots (reserve the pods). Cover and cook over a low heat for 10–15 minutes, stirring from time to time, until the apricots have softened.

Meanwhile, roughly chop the vanilla pod and add to a blender with 3 tablespoons of the sugar. Blend until the vanilla pod is coarsely chopped; set aside.

Pour the vanilla-speckled sugar and remaining sugar into the pan and stir together. Cook over a low heat, stirring from time to time, until the sugar has completely dissolved. Break up some of the fruit with a potato masher if there are still large pieces.

Bring to the boil and boil rapidly for 10–15 minutes, stirring from time to time, until setting point is reached.

Skim off any scum then take off the heat and stir in the butter to disperse any remaining scum, if needed. Ladle the hot jam into warmed sterilised jars right to the top, then screw on lids or cover with waxed discs and cellophane tops secured with elastic bands. Leave to cool, then label and date. Store in a cool place.

Apricot and Marsala jam

This subtle, sophisticated jam is made with a little Marsala wine. Made in Sicily, it is fortified with brandy and has complex flavours of vanilla, brown sugar, apricot and tamarind. Madeira or sweet sherry can be used in its place.

Try this jam swirled through natural yogurt as an easy dessert or mixed with whipped cream to top mini pavlovas or spoon over hot crepes and serve with vanilla ice cream.

1kg apricots, halved, stoned and diced
4 tbsp freshly squeezed orange juice
4 tbsp Marsala wine

1kg jam sugar with added pectin
15g unsalted butter (optional)

Add the diced apricots, orange juice and Marsala to a large china or glass bowl, stir together, then cover and leave to infuse for at least 1 hour.

Tip the apricot mixture into a preserving pan, bring to the boil, then cover and cook over a low heat for 10–15 minutes, stirring from time to time, until the apricots have softened.

Pour in the sugar, stir together, then cook over a low heat, stirring from time to time, until the sugar has completely dissolved. Bring to the boil and boil rapidly for 10–15 minutes, stirring from time to time, until setting point is reached.

Skim off any scum then take off the heat and stir in the butter to disperse any remaining scum, if needed. Ladle the hot jam into warmed sterilised jars right to the top, then screw on lids or cover with waxed discs and cellophane tops secured with elastic bands. Leave to cool, then label and date. Store in a cool place.

Apricots and peaches

Apricots and peaches belong to the rose family, and both are thought to originate in China. Peaches feature in Chinese mythology as a symbol of immortality. The Ancient Greeks and Romans enjoyed apricots, and the name apricot derives from a Latin word for early, or precocious, because they are among the first fruits to come into season. The word 'apricot' also describes their orange-yellow colour; their velvety skin is often tinged red on the side most exposed to the sun.

To be able to grow your own peaches or apricots in chilly Britain was a mark of great wealth and status. Trees can often be found in walled kitchen gardens, where they are sheltered from the wind. At Acorn Bank in Cumbria, there is a beautiful apricot tree that is pollinated by the garden team using a rabbit's tail. But even in a sheltered garden, the unpredictable British climate can be perilous; a glasshouse with tall south-facing windows was the answer for those who could afford it. Waddesdon Manor in Buckinghamshire, built by Baron Ferdinand de Rothschild, has a grand Victorian glasshouse.

Apricots are in our shops and markets for such a short time that you should buy them when you see them. If the fruit that you have is a little on the firm side, apricots and peaches will continue to ripen in a fruit bowl in the kitchen, and will have much more flavour than those kept in the fridge.

Apricots contain medium amounts of pectin, while peaches are low in pectin, so to ensure a good set, use jam sugar with added pectin and boost acidity and flavour with a little orange or lemon juice.

Peach jam

Choose yellow-fleshed peaches for the best flavour and colour; lemon and orange enhance the flavour. There is no need to skin the fruit as the skins will soften during cooking and will be barely noticeable in the finished jam. For a peachy dessert, spoon this jam over crepes, then fold into four, reheat in the pan with a little butter and serve with ice cream for the kids or, for the grown-ups, flame the pancakes while still in the pan with a little warmed orange liqueur or brandy and serve with crème fraîche.

1kg (approx. 8–9) peaches, halved, stoned and diced (no need to peel)
Finely grated zest and juice of 1 lemon
Finely grated zest and juice of 1 small orange or ½ a large one

3 tbsp water
1kg jam sugar with added pectin
15g unsalted butter (optional)

Add the peaches to a preserving pan along with the lemon zest and juice, orange zest and juice and water. Cover and cook over a low heat for about 15 minutes, stirring from time to time, until the peaches have softened.

Pour in the sugar, stir together and continue to cook over a low heat, stirring from time to time, until the sugar has completely dissolved. Bring to the boil and boil rapidly for 10–15 minutes, stirring from time to time, until setting point is reached.

Skim off the scum then take off the heat and stir in the butter to disperse any remaining scum, if needed. Ladle the hot jam into warmed sterilised jars right to the top, then screw on lids or cover with waxed discs and cellophane tops secured with elastic bands. Leave to cool, then label and date. Store in a cool place.

Plum jam with star anise

Star anise adds a fragrant liquorice-aniseed flavour that complements the flavour of the plums. This jam is lovely on toasted sourdough bread for breakfast, or add a tablespoon to the gravy when roasting a duck or casseroling pork.

1.4kg plums, halved, or quartered if
   large, and stoned
4 star anise
150ml water
1.4kg preserving sugar
15g unsalted butter (optional)

Add the plums, star anise and water to a preserving pan, bring to the boil then cover and cook gently for 25–30 minutes, stirring from time to time, until the plums are soft. Crush any large pieces of fruit with a potato masher.

Pour in the sugar, mix together and continue to cook over a low heat, stirring from time to time, until the sugar has completely dissolved. Bring to the boil and boil rapidly for 10–15 minutes, stirring from time to time, until setting point is reached.

Skim off the scum then take off the heat and stir in the butter to disperse any remaining scum if needed. Ladle the hot jam into warmed sterilised jars, adding one star anise to each jar (you will have one jar without one) and ladling the jam right to the top of the jars. Screw on lids or cover with waxed discs and cellophane tops secured with elastic bands. Leave to cool, then label and date. Store in a cool place.

TIP The type of plum that you choose will influence not only the colour of the jam but also how set it will be, as pectin levels vary between plum varieties. For maximum pectin choose fruit that is only just ripe, firm underripe plums can have a bland flavour and the stones can be more difficult to remove. Victoria plums and damsons have long been popular choices.

Strawberry and elderflower jam

What could be more perfect than a spoonful of this on a freshly baked scone with a dollop of clotted cream? Look out for the clusters of creamy white elderflowers from late May to mid-June.

1.4kg strawberries, hulled and halved or quartered depending on size
1.4kg jam sugar with added pectin
Juice of 1½ lemons
6 large open elderflower heads
15g unsalted butter (optional)

Add half the strawberries to a large china or glass bowl, then roughly crush with a potato masher. Add the remaining strawberries, the sugar and lemon juice, and stir together.

Shake the elderflower heads to remove any tiny bugs, then pick off the blossoms (or snip off with scissors) and add to the bowl. Stir together then cover and leave to macerate for 3–4 hours. Stir once or twice to encourage the strawberry juices to run and the sugar to dissolve.

Transfer the mixture to a preserving pan, scraping out the pan with a flexible spatula. Cook over a low heat, stirring from time to time, until the sugar has completely dissolved. Bring to the boil, skim off the scum from around the edges of the pan and boil rapidly for 5–10 minutes, stirring from time to time, until setting point is reached.

Skim off the scum, then take off the heat and stir in the butter to disperse any remaining scum, if needed. Leave the jam for 10 minutes to cool and thicken slightly.

Ladle the hot jam into warmed sterilised jars right to the top, then screw on lids or cover with waxed discs and cellophane tops secured with elastic bands. Leave to cool, then label and date. Store in a cool place.

Blueberry jam

Although blueberries are widely available they can be expensive and you may find it cheaper to use frozen blueberries as here. If using fresh, reduce the amount to 1kg. Blueberries make a very dark jam so don't overboil it as it will darken the colour still further.

1.2kg (3 x 400g packs) frozen
    blueberries
150ml water
Grated zest and juice of 1 lemon
1kg preserving sugar
15g unsalted butter (optional)

Add the blueberries, water, and lemon zest and juice to a preserving pan. Cover and cook over a medium heat for 15–20 minutes, stirring and roughly breaking up the fruit until defrosted and softened.

Stir in the sugar and cook over a low heat until completely dissolved. Bring to the boil and boil rapidly for about 10–15 minutes, stirring from time to time, until setting point is reached.

Skim off the scum then turn off the heat and stir in the butter to disperse any remaining scum, if needed. Leave to stand for 10 minutes. Ladle the hot jam into warmed sterilised jars right to the top then screw on lids or cover with waxed discs and cellophane tops secured with elastic bands. Leave to cool, then label and date. Store in a cool place.

VARIATION You could try making this jam with foraged bilberries.

Cinnamon-spiced bramble and apple jam

During early autumn the National Trust volunteers at Greys Court, Oxfordshire, fill the house with wonderful smells of fruit cooking as they make jam with fruit from the kitchen garden. The last resident of the house was Lady Brunner, a former Chair of the National Federation of Women's Institutes. During the Second World War the Women's Institute played a valuable role in educating women on how to eke out food rations.

This gently spiced jam is full of autumn flavours. If using windfall apples, choose firm apples and cut away any bruised areas. Don't forget to add a bag or plastic container to your backpack when out walking so that you can pick any blackberries that you see. Mashing the fruit during the first cooking will release more blackberry juices so that the apples take on the rich colour of the blackberries.

1.1kg Bramley cooking apples, quartered, cored, peeled and diced
450g blackberries
100ml water
1 tsp ground cinnamon
½ tsp ground ginger
¼ tsp ground cloves
1.4kg preserving sugar
15g unsalted butter (optional)

Add the apples, blackberries and water to a preserving pan then stir in the spices. Bring just to the boil then cover and cook over a low heat for 20–25 minutes, stirring from time to time, until the fruit is soft. Roughly crush the fruit with a potato masher once or twice during this first cooking.

Stir in the sugar and cook over a low heat, stirring from time to time, until the sugar has completely dissolved. Bring to the boil and boil rapidly for 10–15 minutes, stirring from time to time, until setting point is reached.

Skim off the scum then turn off the heat and stir in the butter to disperse any remaining scum, if needed. Ladle the hot jam into warmed sterilised jars right to the top, then screw on lids or cover with waxed discs and cellophane tops secured with elastic bands. Leave to cool, then label and date. Store in a cool place.

Blackcurrant jam

This tangy jam is perfect spread over a toasted crumpet or buttered thick white toast. When making blackcurrant jam it is important that the currants are soft after the first cooking, especially the skins, or they won't soften further once the sugar is added. Test one or two, letting them cool slightly first on a spoon. You should be able to rub the skin from the fruit between your fingers. If you have a very good crop of blackcurrants then you can double up the recipe below. If you don't have any preserving sugar, you can get away with using ordinary granulated sugar.

900g blackcurrants, removed from
    strings
425ml water
1kg preserving sugar
15g unsalted butter (optional)

Add the blackcurrants and water to a preserving pan, bring to the boil then reduce the heat, cover the pan and simmer for about 25 minutes, stirring from time to time, until the currants have softened.

Pour in the sugar, stir together and cook over a low heat, stirring from time to time, until the sugar has completely dissolved.

Bring to the boil and boil rapidly for 10–15 minutes, stirring from time to time, until setting point is reached. Skim off the scum then take the pan off the heat and stir in the butter to disperse any remaining scum, if needed.

Ladle the hot jam into warmed sterilised jars right to the top, then screw on the lids or add waxed discs and cellophane tops secured with elastic bands. Leave to cool, then label and date. Store in a cool place.

TIP Remove currants from their strings by pulling them off with your fingertips or running the tines of a fork through the strings to release the currants.

Redcurrant, strawberry and orange jam

High in pectin, redcurrants are great in jams and jellies as they aid the set and add a lovely pinky red colour, making them the perfect partner to low-pectin strawberries.

As many people aren't sure what to do with redcurrants they can often be found with reduced stickers on them in the supermarket. Buy when you see them and pop the packs in the freezer. Allow 10% more fruit if using frozen.

250g redcurrants, removed from strings

4 tbsp water

1 large orange

750g strawberries, hulled and quartered or diced if large

1kg preserving sugar

15g unsalted butter (optional)

Add the redcurrants and water to a preserving pan. Finely grate the orange zest and add to the redcurrants. Cut the pith away from the orange using a serrated knife, then cut between the membranes to release the orange segments. Reserve the segments, then squeeze the juice from the membrane into the preserving pan. Cover the pan and simmer the redcurrants for 15 minutes until soft, stirring from time to time.

Add the reserved orange segments, strawberries and preserving sugar and cook over a low heat, stirring from time to time, until the sugar has completely dissolved. Bring to the boil and boil rapidly for 10–15 minutes, stirring from time to time, until setting point is reached.

Skim off the scum then turn off the heat and stir in the butter to disperse any remaining scum, if needed. Ladle into warmed sterilised jars right to the top then screw on lids. Leave to cool, then label and date. Store in a cool place.

Traditional summer fruit jam

In many old recipes using fruits that were low in pectin and acid, the jams were boosted by redcurrants, gooseberries or cooking apples. Redcurrants were sometimes cooked in water and strained to make a pectin-rich 'stock syrup'. In this version the redcurrants are left unstrained so that none of the fruit is wasted.

Keeping things traditional, granulated sugar is used; its smaller grains do create a little more scum as the jam boils than preserving or jam sugar. Remove with a skimming spoon or stir in a little butter to break the surface tension and magically make it disappear.

300g redcurrants, removed from strings
3 tbsp water
225g raspberries

500g strawberries, hulled and roughly chopped
1kg granulated sugar
15g unsalted butter (optional)

Add the redcurrants and water to a preserving pan, cover and cook gently for 20 minutes until soft, stirring from time to time and breaking up the fruit with a wooden spoon.

Add the raspberries, strawberries and sugar and mix together. Cook over a low heat, stirring from time to time, until the sugar has completely dissolved. Bring to the boil and boil rapidly for 10–15 minutes, stirring from time to time, until setting point is reached. Skim off the scum then take off the heat and stir in the butter to disperse any remaining scum, if needed. Leave to stand for 10–15 minutes so that the fruit will not rise to the top of the jars when potted.

Ladle into warmed sterilised jars right to the top, then screw on lids or cover with waxed discs and cellophane tops secured with elastic bands. Leave to cool, then label and date. Store in a cool place.

Berry cherry jam

This delicious deep red jam is good added to the bottom of mini sponge puddings, as a filling for jam tarts or spread in the base of a Bakewell or almond frangipane tart.

150g redcurrants, removed from strings
6 tbsp water
450g cherries, stalks removed and stoned

450g strawberries, hulled and roughly chopped
450g raspberries
1.4kg preserving sugar
15g unsalted butter (optional)

Add the redcurrants and water to a preserving pan, cover and cook over a low heat for 15 minutes until soft, crushing with a potato masher from time to time. Press through a sieve into a bowl or jug, then return the redcurrant juice to the preserving pan, discarding the pulp in the sieve.

Add the cherries, strawberries, raspberries and sugar, and cook over a low heat, stirring from time to time, until the sugar has completely dissolved. Crush some of the fruits with a potato masher so that about half are broken up.

Bring to the boil and boil rapidly for 15 minutes, stirring from time to time, until setting point is reached.

Skim off any scum from around the edges of the pan then turn off the heat and stir in the butter to disperse any remaining scum, if needed. Ladle the hot jam into warmed sterilised jars right to the top, then screw on lids or cover with waxed discs and cellophane tops secured with elastic bands. Leave to cool, then label and date. Store in a cool place.

Berries and cherries

Once a traditional English sight, the cherry orchard has been in great decline. In many places where there was once an old orchard now stands a modern housing development with just the name Orchard Way to remind you of the past. With low yields, home-grown cherry producers couldn't compete with cheaper imports from Turkey, Spain and America. However, British cherry growers are staging a comeback with smaller trees that are easier to pick and shielded from the weather in large polytunnels.

Volunteers at the National Trust garden at Lyveden, near Oundle, Northamptonshire, replanted the sixteenth-century orchard almost 20 years ago with a mix of cherries, as well as apples, pears, damsons and walnuts. At Hinton Ampner in Hampshire, you can walk through the cherry orchard in mid-April to enjoy the clusters of double pink flowers from the cherry variety 'Kanzan' that mingle with the snowy blossom of the cherry 'Mount Fuji', which droops almost to the ground in deep clusters. Why not plant a sweet cherry tree in your own garden? The small modern trees can also be trained in a fan shape against a wall or fence. Choose a self-fertile cultivar so that the fruit will not need a pollination partner. Or if you don't have green fingers there are schemes to sponsor a cherry tree and then help with the harvest in orchards around the country.

Redcurrants are generally ready when cherries and summer berries are at their best too. Redcurrants are rich in pectin and can be used to boost pectin levels in berry fruits when making jam.

Gooseberries, redcurrants and blackcurrants all belong to the genus *Ribes*. There are around 20 varieties of gooseberries, all rich in pectin, although only seven varieties are grown commercially by just a handful of farms, and they are almost in danger of disappearing from the shops. The season runs from June to August, with the early tart green gooseberries the first to be harvested. Other varieties yield near white, yellow, green or red berries with a smooth or mildly hairy exterior.

If you have space in your garden or allotment, why not have at a go at growing your own gooseberries? Gooseberry bushes produce a surprisingly large amount of fruit and grow well in most soils, though they are susceptible to frost, so it is best to wrap them in horticultural fleece in the winter, removing it during the day so that pollinating insects can do their bit.

Blueberries originate in North America and most of the blueberries in our shops are imported, although smaller quantities are grown in the UK. The first plants were offered free by a Canadian parson and were snapped up by a Dorset farmer in 1952. The Dorset Blueberry Company is still going strong and other British growers are now on board. Blueberries are hugely popular. Often referred to as a superfood, they contain antioxidants thought to help protect against cancer, heart disease and age-related macular degeneration. Although bear in mind, cooking will reduce some of these benefits.

Don't confuse blueberries with bilberries, which are native to Europe. The species are related and the fruits look similar, although bilberries are slightly smaller, with purple-red pulp. They are acidic and generally are not eaten raw, but they do make good jam and jelly as they are so juicy. Bilberries are not cultivated and can be found growing wild on small wiry shrubs on high ground in Exmoor National Park, the North of England, North Wales and the Wicklow mountains of Ireland. They go under various regional names, such as whortleberry, bulberry, whinberry, or fraughan in Ireland.

Peach Melba jam

Inspired by the French chef Auguste Escoffier's famous dessert, this jam is a mix of peaches, raspberries and vanilla. Try a spoonful of this jam drizzled over a scoop of vanilla ice cream and scattered with a few extra fresh raspberries.

900g (about 7–8) peaches, halved, stoned and diced (no need to skin)
3 tbsp water
½ vanilla pod, sliced

1kg jam sugar with added pectin
115g raspberries
Juice of 1 lemon
15g unsalted butter (optional)

Add the diced peaches and water to a preserving pan, cover and cook over a low heat for about 15 minutes, stirring from time to time, until the peaches have softened.

Meanwhile, add the sliced vanilla to a food processor or blender with 3 tablespoons of the sugar and blend until the vanilla is finely chopped. Add to the preserving pan along with the remaining sugar, the raspberries and the lemon juice, and mix together. Cook over a low heat, stirring from time to time, until the sugar has completely dissolved.

Bring to the boil and boil rapidly for 10–15 minutes, stirring from time to time, until setting point is reached. Skim off the scum then take off the heat and stir in the butter to disperse any remaining scum, if needed. Leave the jam to stand for 10 minutes so that the pieces of peach don't rise to the top of the jars.

Ladle into warmed sterilised jars right to the top, then screw on lids or cover with waxed discs and cellophane tops secured with elastic bands. Leave to cool, then label and date. Store in a cool place.

Citrussy dried fig preserve

This spicy festive preserve smells delightful as it bubbles on the hob. It would make a lovely Christmas gift and tastes great spooned over toasted teacakes or English muffins.

2 large oranges
1 lemon
200g dried figs, cut into small dice
1.1kg Bramley cooking apples,
    quartered, cored, peeled and diced
2.5cm piece of fresh ginger, peeled
    and finely chopped

1 tsp ground cinnamon
100ml water
1kg preserving sugar
400g light muscovado sugar
15g unsalted butter (optional)

Coarsely grate the orange and lemon zest then squeeze the juice. Cut the squeezed fruit halves into quarters then tie in a square of muslin, along with any pips. Add the zest, juice and muslin bag to a preserving pan.

Add the dried figs, apples, ginger, cinnamon and water and stir together. Bring to the boil then cover and simmer for 25–30 minutes, stirring from time to time, until the apples are softened.

Using a wooden spoon, lift the muslin bag out of the fruit mix and, holding it above the pan, press the liquid out with a second wooden spoon so that it falls into the pan. Alternatively, transfer the muslin bag to a sieve set over a bowl, press the juice into the bowl then add to the preserving pan. Discard the muslin bag.

Stir in the sugars and cook over a low heat, stirring from time to time, until the sugars have completely dissolved. Bring to the boil and boil rapidly for 10–15 minutes, stirring from time to time, until setting point is reached.

Skim off the scum then take the pan off the heat and stir in the butter to disperse any remaining scum if needed. Ladle the hot jam into warmed sterilised jars right to the top, then screw on lids or cover with waxed discs and cellophane tops secured with elastic bands. Leave to cool, then label and date. Store in a cool place.

Peach jam with rosé wine

This jam captures the joy of a Mediterranean summer for you to re-live during the grey days of winter. Don't keep it just for toast; use it to sandwich a Victoria sponge or to top rice pudding.

Choose ripe peaches, but not bruised ones. If slightly underripe, increase the initial cooking time by 5–10 minutes and cook over a low heat until the peaches are really nice and soft.

1kg ripe peaches (6–7 large or 8–9 small), halved, stoned and diced (no need to skin)
150ml rosé wine

1kg jam sugar with added pectin
Juice of 1 lemon
15g unsalted butter (optional)

Add the diced peaches and wine to a large china or glass bowl, stir together, then cover and leave to infuse for at least 1 hour.

Transfer the peaches and wine to a preserving pan, bring to the boil, then cover and cook gently for about 15 minutes, stirring from time to time, until the peaches are soft.

Add the sugar and lemon juice, mix together and cook over a gentle heat, stirring from time to time, until the sugar has completely dissolved. Bring to the boil and boil rapidly for 5–10 minutes, stirring from time to time, until setting point is reached.

Skim off the scum then take the pan off the heat and stir in the butter to disperse any remaining scum, if needed. Leave the jam to stand for 10 minutes. Ladle into warmed sterilised jars right to the top, then screw on lids or cover with waxed discs and cellophane tops secured with elastic bands. Leave to cool, then label and date. Store in a cool place.

Greengage and almond jam

Greengages are a member of the plum family. Their season is short, so look out for home-grown gages in August and September. Greengage jam is a pretty pale green in the jar, but is almost translucent when spooned over bread and butter. Leave the finished jam to stand for 10 minutes before potting, so that the almonds are evenly distributed through the jam and don't all float to the top.

1.4kg greengages, halved and stoned
6 tbsp water
1.4kg preserving sugar

25g flaked almonds
15g unsalted butter (optional)

Add the greengages and water to a preserving pan, bring to the boil then cover and cook over a low heat for 25–30 minutes, stirring from time to time, until the fruit is soft. Break up any larger pieces of fruit with a potato masher, if needed.

Pour in the sugar, stir together and cook over a low heat, stirring from time to time, until the sugar has completely dissolved. Bring to the boil and boil rapidly for 10–15 minutes, stirring from time to time, until setting point is reached.

Skim off the scum then take the pan off the heat and stir in the almonds and butter to disperse any remaining scum if needed. Leave to stand for 10 minutes. Stir again then ladle the hot jam into warmed sterilised jars right to the top, then screw on lids or cover with waxed discs and cellophane tops secured with elastic bands. Leave to cool, then label and date. Store in a cool place.

TIP Choose fruit that is just ripe and juicy. If the fruit is very firm, increase the amounts by 110g for every 450g of fruit used, increasing the amount of water to 4 tablespoons for every 450g of fruit.

Gooseberry and lemon geranium jam

Scented geraniums are popular plants for a sunny conservatory. Don't confuse them with the window box-style geraniums with large round leaves and brightly coloured flowers. Scented geraniums can be recognised by gently pressing the leaves to release the scent; different varieties smell of fruits, spices or roses.

900g gooseberries, topped and tailed
300ml water
4 lemon geranium leaves (optional)

1kg preserving sugar
15g unsalted butter (optional)

Add the gooseberries, water and lemon geranium leaves, if using, to a preserving pan. Bring to the boil, cover and cook over a low heat for 20–25 minutes until the fruit is soft, stirring from time to time.

Pour in the sugar and cook over a low heat, stirring from time to time, until the sugar has completely dissolved. Bring to the boil and boil rapidly for 10–15 minutes, stirring from time to time, until setting point is reached.

Skim off the scum then turn off the heat and remove the lemon geranium leaves, if used. Stir in the butter to disperse any remaining scum, if needed. Ladle the hot jam into warmed sterilised jars right to the top, then screw on lids or cover with waxed discs and cellophane tops secured with elastic bands. Leave to cool, then label and date. Store in a cool place.

VARIATION Instead of lemon geranium leaves, add 3–4 elderflower heads to the gooseberries when cooking, but remove them before adding the sugar.

Red gooseberry and strawberry jam

Red gooseberries are much sweeter than their green counterparts
and their rosy colour blends well with strawberries. Naturally high
in pectin, they boost the lower levels found in strawberries. Red
gooseberries don't lose their colour after cooking. Add to preserves,
pies, crumbles, fools or sorbet, or make into tangy sauces. The
French for gooseberry is *groseille* à *maquereau* or 'mackerel
currant', as it makes a good sauce to go with grilled mackerel.

680g red gooseberries, topped and
   tailed
4 tbsp water
340g strawberries, hulled and
   quartered or diced if large

1kg preserving sugar
15g unsalted butter (optional)

Add the gooseberries and water to a preserving pan, cover and cook
over a low heat for about 20 minutes, stirring from time to time, until
the gooseberries are soft.

Stir in the strawberries and sugar, and cook over a low heat, stirring
from time to time, until the sugar has completely dissolved. Bring to
the boil and boil rapidly for 10–15 minutes, stirring from time to time,
until setting point is reached.

Skim off the scum then turn off the heat and stir in the butter to
disperse any remaining scum, if needed. Leave to stand for 15 minutes
so that the strawberries are evenly distributed through the jam and
don't all float to the top.

Ladle into warmed sterilised jars right to the top, then screw on lids
or cover with waxed discs and cellophane tops and secure with elastic
bands. Leave to cool, then label and date. Store in a cool place.

Ruby grapefruit and raspberry jam

This preserve is rather like a cross between a jam and a marmalade – perfect to spread over breakfast toast. As you peel the grapefruit, work over a large chopping board and tip the juices into the preserving pan from time to time. The grapefruit peel, pith and pips contain valuable pectin, so save them, tie in muslin and cook with the grapefruit flesh.

3 ruby grapefruit	1kg preserving sugar
250g raspberries	15g unsalted butter (optional)

Put a chopping board inside a large Swiss roll tin so that you can catch the grapefruit juice as you prepare the fruit. Cut the peel and pith away from the grapefruit with a serrated knife and put to one side with any pips, pouring the juice into a preserving pan. You should have about 750g peeled weight of grapefruit. Cut the peeled fruit into quarters and cut away the central white core then chop the flesh, including the membrane that holds the grapefruit segments together. Add to the preserving pan with the juice from the tin; there will be a lot of juice, so you will not need to add any extra water.

Put the reserved grapefruit pith, peel, pips and white core on a large square of muslin, then draw up the edges, tie with string and add to the preserving pan. Cover the pan and cook over a low heat for 20 minutes until the fruit is soft. Put the muslin bag in a ladle and use a wooden spoon to press out the juices so that they fall back into the pan. Discard the bag.

Add the raspberries and sugar to the pan, stir together, then heat gently, stirring from time to time, until the sugar has completely dissolved. Bring to the boil and boil rapidly for 10–15 minutes, stirring from time to time, until setting point is reached.

Skim off the scum then turn off the heat and stir in the butter to disperse any remaining scum, if needed. Ladle the hot jam into warmed sterilised jars right to the top, then screw on lids or cover with waxed discs and cellophane tops and secure with elastic bands. Leave to cool, then label and date. Store in a cool place.

Tropical pineapple and mango jam

In the 1800s the Walled Garden at Shugborough Estate in Staffordshire was at the forefront of farming technology and the gardeners could grow pineapple on its steam-heated walls. Both pineapples and mangoes are low in pectin, jam's natural setting agent. Jam sugar has added pectin and lime juice boosts acidity.

1 large pineapple, peeled, reserving the juices

1 large mango, stoned, peeled and cut into chunks

Grated zest and juice of 2 limes

4 tbsp water

1kg jam sugar with added pectin

15g unsalted butter (optional)

Use a small knife to remove any small brown 'eyes' from the pineapple, then cut it in quarters vertically to give four wedges. Cut the central core away from each wedge then cut the flesh into small dice. Add to a preserving pan with any juice.

Add the mango chunks to the preserving pan.

Add the lime zest and juice and the water, cover the pan and cook over a low heat for 20 minutes until soft.

Stir in the sugar then cook over a low heat, stirring from time to time, until the sugar has completely dissolved. Bring to the boil and boil rapidly for 10–15 minutes, stirring from time to time, until setting point is reached.

Skim off the scum then turn off the heat and stir in the butter to disperse any remaining scum, if needed. Ladle the hot jam into warmed sterilised jars right to the top, then screw on lids or cover with waxed discs and cellophane tops secured with elastic bands. Leave to cool, then label and date. Store in a cool place.

Rhubarb, ginger and orange jam

This is a chunky jam. If you prefer a finer texture, blitz the orange and ginger in a food processor.

1kg trimmed rhubarb, cut into 2cm
  slices
1.1kg preserving or granulated sugar
Grated zest and juice of 1 lemon
1 large orange

600ml water
55g drained stem ginger in syrup
  (about 3 pieces), finely chopped
15g unsalted butter (optional)

Layer the rhubarb, sugar and lemon zest in a large glass or china bowl, then drizzle with the lemon juice, cover and leave in a cool place overnight. Stir before you go to bed and again in the morning.

Put the orange in a small saucepan, pour in the water and bring to the boil. Cover and simmer for 1 hour or until the orange is very tender. If the water doesn't cover the orange then turn it several times during cooking so that it cooks evenly. Leave to cool in the pan and set aside until next day.

Transfer the rhubarb and sugar mix to a preserving pan, scraping out every last bit with a flexible spatula, and cook over a low heat, stirring from time to time, until the sugar has completely dissolved.

Drain and finely chop the orange, discarding the cooking water, and add the orange to the preserving pan with the ginger. Bring the mixture to the boil and boil rapidly for 10–15 minutes, stirring from time to time, until setting point is reached.

Skim off the scum then turn off the heat and stir in the butter to disperse any scum, if needed. Ladle the hot jam into warmed sterilised jars right to the top, then screw on lids or cover with waxed discs and cellophane tops secured with elastic bands. Leave to cool, then label and date. Store in a cool place.

High Dumpsie Dearie jam

No one really knows the origin of its name but this old recipe was found in the Women's Institute archives. This is a version of a favourite orchard fruit jam made with mixed plums, pears and apples, and flavoured with ginger and lemon. If you prefer, you can swap the diced pear for the same weight of prepared marrow.

450g (or about 2) Bramley cooking
   apples, peeled, cored and diced
450g (or about 4–5 small) Conference
   pears, peeled, cored and diced
450g Victoria plums, or other
   red-skinned plums, stoned and
   quartered

300ml water
1.4kg preserving sugar
40g drained stem ginger in syrup,
   finely chopped
Grated zest and juice of 1 lemon
15g unsalted butter (optional)

Add the apples, pears and plums to a preserving pan, pour in the water and bring just to the boil. Cover and cook over a low heat for 25–30 minutes, stirring from time to time, until the fruit is soft. The apples and plums will break down with the diced pear remaining in neat cubes.

Add the sugar, ginger and lemon zest and juice, and stir together. Cook over a low heat, stirring from time to time, until the sugar has completely dissolved. Bring to the boil and boil rapidly for 10–15 minutes, stirring from time to time, until setting point is reached.

Skim then take the pan off the heat and stir in the butter to disperse any remaining scum, if needed. Leave to stand for 10 minutes.

Ladle the hot jam into warmed sterilised jars right to the top, then screw on lids or cover with waxed discs and cellophane tops secured with elastic bands. Leave to cool, then label and date. Store in a cool place.

Minted marrow and blackberry jam

If you have ever grown marrows you will know how prolific they are. Many cooks have come up with ingenious ways of using up a glut. Traditional marrow jams were often flavoured with ginger; this version adds fruity blackberries and zingy lemon juice with Bramley apples to aid the set. To prepare the marrow, cut off the stalk and then cut away the skin. Cut in half and scoop out the seeds and fibrous centre using a dessert spoon.

400g prepared marrow, cut into small dice
500g (or about 2) Bramley cooking apples, peeled, cored and cut into small dice
500g blackberries

Finely grated zest and juice of 1 lemon
120ml water
1kg granulated sugar
5 tsp finely chopped fresh mint (optional)
15g unsalted butter (optional)

Add the marrow, apple and blackberries to a preserving pan, add the lemon zest and juice and stir in the water. Cover and cook over a low heat for 30 minutes, stirring from time to time, until the fruit is soft.

Stir in the sugar and cook over a low heat, stirring from time to time, until the sugar has completely dissolved. Bring to the boil and boil rapidly for 10–15 minutes, stirring from time to time, until setting point is reached. Skim off the scum then turn off the heat and stir in the mint, if using, and the butter to remove any remaining scum, if needed.

Ladle the hot jam into warmed sterilised jars right to the top then screw on lids or cover with waxed discs and cellophane tops secured with elastic bands. Leave to cool, then label and date. Store in a cool place.

Conserves and reduced-sugar jams

Reduced-sugar strawberry jam

Strawberry jam is often regarded as the most difficult jam to make. The delicate fruits are high in water and low in pectin, the natural setting agent, so if you don't cook it for long enough the jam won't set enough to stay on your bread; too long and the vibrant red colour will become a rather dismal poor relation. You may wonder, why make life more difficult by attempting to cook a reduced-sugar version?

Mashing the strawberries releases the juices, drawing the water out and speeding up the sugar dissolving. Grated cooking apple boosts pectin levels. As the pectin in the fruit is released and mixed with the added pectin in the jam sugar, the acidity from the lemon juice helps to produces a gel. With lower sugar levels this jam will have a fairly soft texture. As the pieces of strawberry are small the jam can be potted without leaving it to stand.

1.1kg strawberries, hulled and halved
   or quartered if large
300g (or 1 large) Bramley
   cooking apple, peeled,
   cored and coarsely grated

Juice of 1 lemon
700g jam sugar with added pectin
15g unsalted butter (optional)

Add the strawberries to a preserving pan and roughly crush with a potato masher. Add the grated apple, lemon juice and sugar, and stir together. Cook over a low heat, stirring and crushing the fruit with the potato masher, until the sugar has completely dissolved.

Bring to the boil and boil rapidly for about 10 minutes, stirring from time to time, until setting point is reached. Skim once during boiling, if needed, then take off the heat and stir in the butter to disperse any remaining scum, if needed.

Ladle the hot jam into warmed sterilised jars right to the top, then screw on lids or cover with waxed discs and cellophane tops secured with elastic bands. Leave to cool, then label and date. Store in the fridge for up to one month.

VARIATION You might like to add a few crushed black peppercorns, a little rose water or a few dried lavender petals to the finished jam along with the butter.

Black cherry conserve

There are only three ingredients in this luxurious conserve, packed with pieces of juicy cherries – so you need really good cherries. Leave the conserve to stand for 10–15 minutes before spooning into jars. This will allow it to thicken slightly, so that the pieces of cherry don't rise to the top. If you have some kirsch or cherry brandy you might like to add 2 teaspoons to the warmed jars before potting the hot conserve, but don't be overly generous or the conserve will be too runny when cold.

1kg just-ripe black cherries, stoned
800g preserving sugar

Juice of 1 lemon
15g unsalted butter (optional)

Layer the cherries and sugar in a large china or glass dish. Drizzle over the lemon juice then cover and leave at room temperature overnight. Stir the mixture once or twice to encourage the cherry juices to run and the sugar to dissolve.

The next day, stir the mixture well, then scoop into a preserving pan, using a flexible spatula to scrape every last bit of sugar out of the dish. Cook over a low heat, stirring from time to time, until the sugar has completely dissolved.

Bring to the boil and boil rapidly for 10–15 minutes, stirring from time to time, until setting point is reached. Take the pan off the heat and stir in the butter, if needed, to disperse any scum. Leave to stand for 10–15 minutes.

Ladle into warmed sterilised jars right to the top, then screw on lids or cover with waxed discs and cellophane tops secured with elastic bands. Leave to cool, then label and date. Store in a cool place.

Gingered pear and saffron conserve

At Bateman's, the former East Sussex home of Rudyard Kipling, you will find a beautiful arched walkway known as the Pear Allée.

1.4kg just-ripe Conference pears, quartered, cored and cut into small dice
Finely grated zest and juice of 1 lemon
120ml water
Large pinch of saffron threads

50g fresh ginger, peeled and finely chopped
3 cardamom pods, crushed, seeds finely ground (optional)
1kg jam sugar with added pectin
15g unsalted butter (optional)

Add the pears, lemon zest and juice and water to a preserving pan and mix together. Stir in the saffron, ginger and cardamom pods and seeds, if using, and bring to the boil. Cover and cook over a low heat for 20–25 minutes, stirring from time to time, until the pears are tender.

Pour in the sugar, stir and cook over a low heat, stirring from time to time, until the sugar has completely dissolved. Break up some of the pieces of fruit with a potato masher if you prefer a smoother conserve.

Bring to the boil and boil rapidly for about 10 minutes, stirring from time to time, until setting point is reached. Take off the heat, remove the green cardamom pods and stir in the butter to disperse any remaining scum, if needed. Leave to stand for 10–15 minutes so that the pears will not float to the surface.

Ladle the hot jam into warmed sterilised jars right to the top, then screw on lids or cover with waxed discs and cellophane tops secured with elastic bands. Leave to cool, then label and date. Store in a cool place.

Reduced-sugar kiwi fruit jam

Native to China, when kiwi fruit were first introduced to New Zealand in 1904 they were known as Chinese gooseberries. They later became known as kiwi fruit because their brown fuzzy skins resemble the flightless native New Zealand bird known as a kiwi. Rich in vitamin C and other powerful antioxidants, the kiwi fruit is a great way to boost our five a day. For jam making, choose firm and just-ripe fruit.

1.1kg (about 15) kiwi fruit, halved
Grated zest and juice of 1 large lime

500g jam sugar with added pectin
15g unsalted butter (optional)

Working over a bowl to catch all the juice, scoop the kiwi flesh from the skins using a teaspoon. Tip the juice into a preserving pan. Divide the fruit in half, scooping out the largest pieces onto a chopping board. Tip the rest into the preserving pan, add the lime zest and juice, then cook over a low heat for 5 minutes, mashing the fruit with a potato masher until soft.

Chop the rest of the fruit, add to the pan then stir in the sugar. Cook over a low heat, stirring from time to time, until the sugar has completely dissolved. Bring to the boil and boil rapidly for 5–10 minutes, stirring frequently, until setting point is reached. Take off the heat and stir in the butter, if needed, to disperse any remaining scum.

Ladle the hot jam into warmed sterilised jars right to the top, then screw on lids or cover with waxed discs and cellophane tops secured with elastic bands. Leave to cool, then label and date. Store in the fridge for up to one month.

Plum and prune conserve

Prunes are dried plums, and they add depth and concentrated flavour to this conserve. For convenience buy ready-pitted prunes. If you do buy them with their stones in, weigh the prunes after you have taken them out. These days it's easy to buy soft prunes that are ready to eat.

Choose red plums for the best colour, ideally the British favourite Victoria plums, but their season is short. If you are using larger imported plums, halve and stone the plums and cut each half in half again.

1kg just-ripe plums, halved and stoned

100g ready-to-eat pitted prunes, cut into small dice

150ml water

700g granulated or preserving sugar

175g light muscovado sugar

15g unsalted butter (optional)

Add the plums, prunes and water to a preserving pan, bring to the boil, then cover and cook over a low heat for 25–30 minutes, stirring from time to time, until the plums are soft.

Pour in the white and brown sugar, stir together and cook over a low heat, stirring from time to time, until the sugars have completely dissolved. Bring to the boil and boil rapidly for 10–15 minutes, stirring from time to time, until setting point is reached. Take off the heat and stir in the butter, if needed, to disperse any remaining scum.

Ladle the hot jam into warmed sterilised jars right to the top, then screw on lids or cover with waxed discs and cellophane tops secured with elastic bands. Leave to cool, then label and date. Store in a cool place.

Reduced-sugar nectarine jam

Nectarines are genetically almost identical to peaches: the gene that separates them determines the smooth skin of a nectarine rather than the velvety skin of a peach. Both fruits can have yellow or white flesh, and either can be used in this recipe. With nectarines, the red blush to their skins adds a reddish tinge to the finished jam, with chunky pieces of yellow flesh. Choose just-ripe nectarines for the best flavour.

1kg (approx. 10–11) nectarines, halved and stoned
Juice of 1 lemon

4 tbsp water
500g jam sugar with added pectin
15g unsalted butter (optional)

Finely dice the nectarines and add to a preserving pan with the lemon juice and water. Cover and cook over a low heat for 10–15 minutes, stirring from time to time with a wooden spoon, until the fruit has softened.

Stir in the sugar and cook over a low heat, stirring from time to time, until the sugar has completely dissolved. Bring to the boil and boil rapidly for 5–10 minutes, stirring from time to time, until setting point is reached. Take the pan off the heat and stir in the butter, if needed, to disperse any remaining scum. Break up the fruit slightly with a potato masher if you prefer a finer textured jam.

Ladle the hot jam into warmed sterilised jars right to the top, then screw on lids or cover with waxed discs and cellophane tops secured with elastic bands. Leave to cool, then label and date. Store in the fridge for up to one month.

Mango and melon reduced-sugar jam

This sunny-coloured conserve has a delicate flavour with a zing of lime that is great on toast or warm croissants. For the best colour, choose an orange-fleshed cantaloupe or Charentais melon.

---

2 large just-ripe mangoes, stoned, peeled and cut into small dice
Grated zest and juice of 2 large limes
Juice of 1 lemon
4 tbsp water

1 cantaloupe melon, halved, deseeded, peeled and cut into small dice
600g jam sugar with added pectin
15g unsalted butter (optional)

Add the diced mangoes, lime zest and juice, lemon juice and water to a preserving pan, cover and cook over a low heat for about 5 minutes until the fruit has softened.

Add the melon and sugar, and stir together. Cook over a low heat, stirring from time to time, until the sugar has completely dissolved. Mash the fruit lightly with a potato masher.

Bring to the boil and boil rapidly for 10–15 minutes, stirring from time to time, until setting point is reached. Turn off the heat and stir in the butter, if needed, to disperse any remaining scum. Leave to stand for 10–15 minutes until slightly thickened.

Ladle the warm jam into warmed sterilised jars right to the top, then screw on lids or cover with waxed discs and cellophane tops secured with elastic bands. Leave to cool, then label and date. Store for up to one month in the fridge.

TIP You may find that this jam takes a few more minutes to come to setting point than some of the other conserves. Leave the conserve to cool for 10–15 minutes before potting so that the fruit doesn't rise in the jar. If it does – and you have screwed the lids on tightly – turn the jar upside down for a minute or two.

Reduced-sugar apricot and cardamom jam

Cardamom has an exotic perfume that goes well with the delicate flavour of apricots. The flavour can be intense, so start with just two crushed pods and then taste the jam once the sugar has dissolved. If you would like a slightly stronger flavour, add one more cardamom pod and then boil the jam.

1kg apricots, quartered and stoned
Juice of 1 orange
2–3 green cardamom pods, crushed, seeds finely ground

4 tbsp water
500g jam sugar with added pectin
15g unsalted butter (optional)

Add the apricots to a preserving pan with the orange juice, cardamom pods and seeds and water. Cover and cook over a low heat for 10–15 minutes, stirring with a wooden spoon from time to time, until the apricots have softened.

Stir in the sugar and cook over a low heat, stirring from time to time, until the sugar has completely dissolved.

Bring to the boil and boil rapidly for 5–10 minutes, stirring from time to time, until setting point is reached. Take off the heat, remove the green cardamom pods and stir in the butter if needed, to disperse any remaining scum.

Break up any larger pieces of apricot with a potato masher, if liked, then ladle the hot jam into warmed sterilised jars right to the top and screw on lids or cover with waxed discs and cellophane tops secured with elastic bands. Leave to cool, then label and date. Store in the fridge for up to one month.

Greengage and apple conserve

This fresh-tasting conserve has a citrus tang, great for breakfast on a toasted bagel or wholewheat toast.

Sir Thomas Gage of Hengrave Hall, Suffolk, brought the first greengages to Britain from France in the eighteenth century. Their mottled green skin may suggest that these fruits are a little on the sharp side, but they are naturally sweet. Bite into a ripe fruit and the honey-like juices will almost certainly dribble down your chin.

1.1kg greengages, halved, stoned and chopped
300g (or 1) Bramley cooking apple, quartered, cored, peeled and diced
Grated zest and juice of ½ orange

Grated zest and juice of 1 lemon
4 tbsp water
800g preserving sugar
15g unsalted butter (optional)

Add the greengages, apple and orange and lemon zest and juice to a preserving pan, spoon in the water and stir together. Bring to the boil then cover and cook over a low heat for 15–20 minutes, stirring from time to time, until the fruit has softened.

Pour in the sugar, stir, and cook over a low heat, stirring from time to time, until the sugar has completely dissolved.

Bring to the boil and boil rapidly for 10–15 minutes, stirring from time to time, until setting point is reached. Turn off the heat and stir in the butter to disperse any remaining scum, if needed. Ladle the hot jam into warmed sterilised jars right to the top, then screw on lids or cover with waxed discs and cellophane tops secured with elastic bands. Leave to cool, then label and date. Store in a cool place.

Figs

One of the earliest fruits to be cultivated by man, figs are native to Western Asia and spread to countries around the Mediterranean. Early Olympic athletes used figs as a training food and in ancient Roman times they were believed to increase strength in young people while helping to stave off signs of ageing in older people.

Fig trees have no blossom on their branches: the blossom is inside the fruit, where the many tiny flowers become the crunchy edible seeds that give figs their unique flavour. In good climates a fig tree can grow to 5–9 metres tall and bear two crops in a year. Figs can be grown in Britain but need a sheltered spot and they are often grown against the wall in a kitchen garden or large greenhouse. It used to be said that they should be grown in a Gladstone bag to prevent them growing too big; a large pot or bucket would work in the same way to compress the roots.

Beningbrough Hall in Yorkshire is a grand house dating from 1716, famed for its collection of art, with a large walled kitchen garden and separate orchard. It is still very much a working garden, supplying fruit and vegetables to the café. With many varieties of fruit, from figs and grapes to pears, and over 50 types of apple, there is always something just coming into season. The purple-skinned variety of fig known as 'Brown Turkey' is so prolific that the figs are offered to the staff and public to raise money for a local charity.

Honeyed fig conserve

This is a luxurious conserve and well worth the expense of a vanilla pod for its wonderful flavour. Honey was used in the earliest jams; here it is mixed with jam sugar to get a good set, with the lovely taste of honey. If available, choose dark purple-skinned figs for the best coloured jam.

1kg (about 10–11 large) fresh figs, stalks trimmed off, roughly chopped
Finely grated zest and juice of 2 lemons

120ml water
1 vanilla pod
750g jam sugar with added pectin
100g honey (runny or thick set)

Add the figs, lemon zest and juice and water to a preserving pan. Slit the vanilla pod lengthways, scrape out the soft black seeds and add to the pan. Bring the liquid just to the boil, then cover the pan and cook over a low heat for about 15 minutes, stirring from time to time and breaking up some of the larger pieces of fruit, until the figs are soft.

Meanwhile, roughly chop the vanilla pod and add to a blender with 3 tablespoons of the sugar. Blend until the vanilla is finely chopped; set aside.

Pour the vanilla-speckled sugar and the remaining sugar and honey into the pan and cook over a low heat, stirring from time to time, until the sugar has completely dissolved. Bring to the boil and boil rapidly for about 10 minutes, stirring from time to time, until setting point is reached.

Ladle into warmed sterilised jars right to the top, then screw on lids or cover with waxed discs and cellophane tops secured with elastic bands. Leave to cool, then label and date. Store in a cool place.

Red berry trio conserve

Jam making is a good way to use produce from the garden or allotment. But what if you don't have either? This recipe is based on supermarket packs of fruit. Raspberries and strawberries seem to be available all year round with imported crops; look out for home-grown red berries from mid-May onwards. Rich in pectin and natural fruit acids, gooseberries make a great partner for lower pectin red summer berries. Green gooseberries are generally in the shops from June onwards, but to maintain the lovely deep red of this conserve, seek out sweeter red gooseberries; you may find them in some supermarkets or local farmers markets.

450g red gooseberries, topped and tailed
100ml water
800g strawberries, hulled and quartered or chopped if very large
250g raspberries
1.1kg preserving sugar
15g unsalted butter (optional)

Add the gooseberries and water to a preserving pan, bring the water just to the boil then cover and cook over a low heat for 20–25 minutes until the gooseberries are very soft. Crush any large berries with a potato masher if needed.

Mix in the strawberries and raspberries then add the sugar. Cook over a low heat, stirring from time to time, until the sugar has completely dissolved. Bring to the boil and boil rapidly for 10–15 minutes, stirring from time to time, until setting point is reached.

Skim off the scum then take the pan off the heat and stir in the butter to disperse any remaining scum, if needed. Ladle the hot jam into warmed sterilised jars right to the top, then screw on lids or cover with waxed discs and cellophane tops secured with elastic bands. Leave to cool, then label and date. Store in a cool place.

Raspberries

Cultivated in Britain since the seventeenth century, raspberries belong to the same family as the blackberry and the rose. Each raspberry is made up of around 100 drupelets, containing juicy pulp and a seed. The ancient Romans believed that raspberries had medicinal properties and modern midwives still advise pregnant women to drink raspberry leaf tea to speed up the second stage of labour.

Once picked, raspberries do not continue to ripen and are highly perishable. In Victorian and Edwardian times, the head gardeners of big houses had their work cut out as raspberries became increasingly popular for cordials, fruit vinegars, refreshing soft drinks, desserts and sauces. In a bid to impress their employers and neighbouring estates new fruits began to appear. The loganberry is a cross between a raspberry and a blackberry, the boysenberry is a cross between a raspberry, blackberry and loganberry, while the nessberry is a cross between a dewberry, raspberry and blackberry. These varieties unfortunately are not available in the shops but can be grown in the garden at home.

In the 1950s the very best raspberries came from Scotland; they were transported down to London on a steam train known as 'The Raspberry Special'.

Although we think of raspberries as always being red, there are over 200 varieties, some of which are pale yellow, gold, purple and black, with gold being the sweetest.

Reduced-sugar raspberry jam

In this jam, half the raspberries are crushed and then pressed through a sieve. This removes many of the seeds, which to some people are the most irritating thing about raspberry jam.

1kg raspberries
Juice of 1 lemon
500g jam sugar with added pectin
15g unsalted butter (optional)

Add half the raspberries to a preserving pan with the lemon juice and roughly crush with a potato masher. Cook over a low heat for 5 minutes, crushing and stirring from time to time with the potato masher.

Tip the fruit mixture into a sieve set over a bowl and press the fruit pulp through the sieve. Discard the seeds. Pour the purée back into the preserving pan and reheat.

Stir in the sugar then add the remaining raspberries and cook over a low heat, stirring from time to time, until the sugar has completely dissolved. Bring to the boil and boil rapidly for 5–10 minutes, stirring from time to time, until setting point is reached.

Take off the heat and stir in the butter to disperse any remaining scum, if needed. Ladle the hot jam into warmed sterilised jars right to the top, then screw on lids. Leave to cool, then label and date. Store in the fridge for up to 1 month.

Red grape and spiced red wine conserve

Cooking grapes with a little cinnamon, cloves, orange and lemon gives this conserve the flavour of mulled wine. It is the perfect winter choice on toasted teacakes or crumpets. At Beningbrough Hall, North Yorkshire, grapes are grown in the walled kitchen garden and in the glasshouse to extend the season.

1kg red seedless grapes, taken from stems and halved

120ml red wine

Finely grated zest and juice of ½ small orange

Finely grated zest and juice of 1 lemon

5cm piece of cinnamon stick

4 cloves

750g preserving sugar

15g unsalted butter (optional)

Add the grapes, wine and orange and lemon zest and juice to a preserving pan, then add the cinnamon and cloves. Bring just to the boil then cover the pan and cook over a low heat for about 15 minutes until the grapes are soft.

Stir in the sugar and cook over a low heat, stirring from time to time, until the sugar has completely dissolved.

Bring to the boil and boil rapidly for about 15 minutes, stirring from time to time, until setting point is reached. Turn off the heat and stir in the butter to disperse any remaining scum, if needed. Discard the cinnamon stick and cloves (if you can find them).

Ladle the hot jam into warmed sterilised jars right to the top, then screw on lids or cover with waxed discs and cellophane tops secured with elastic bands. Leave to cool, then label and date. Store in a cool place.

Cheat's blackberry and chia conserve

This preserve uses frozen blackberries and it isn't boiled with sugar like a traditional jam. So how does it set? Well the trendy new ingredient, chia seeds, magically create a gel, as these strange little black seeds can absorb ten times their weight in liquid. This preserve is made with a very small amount of sugar, just 2–3 tablespoons of honey or another sweetener such as agave syrup, maple syrup or light muscovado sugar. With such low amounts of sugar, purists may argue that this is a fruit spread rather than a conserve. Serve this fruity conserve on hot toast or spooned over porridge, or top bircher-style muesli with some natural yogurt and a large spoonful of conserve.

450g frozen blackberries	3 tbsp chia seeds
2–3 tbsp honey or sweetener of choice	¼ tsp vanilla extract (optional)

Add the blackberries to a saucepan, cover and cook over a low heat for 5–10 minutes, stirring from time to time, until the blackberries have defrosted and the juices have begun to run.

Stir in 2 tablespoons of honey or other sweetener and the chia seeds and increase the heat slightly. Continue to cook for 3–5 minutes, stirring constantly and breaking up the blackberries with a wooden spoon, until the mixture has thickened and gelled.

Take off the heat, stir in the vanilla, if using, and leave to stand for a minute or two. Taste and stir in a little extra honey or your favourite sweetener, if needed. Ladle into a warmed sterilised jar, screw on the lid and leave to cool. Label and date, and store in the fridge for up to 7 days.

Reduced-sugar blueberry and lime jam

With 40% less sugar than a traditional jam, this rich dark jam is full of fruity flavour. Lime zest and juice really bring the jam alive and aid setting, too. Take the limes out of the fridge for a few hours before using them: warmer fruits will yield more juice than very cold ones. Less sugar does mean that this jam must be kept in the fridge. Try serving on toasted cinnamon bagels spread with a little cream cheese, or with warmed croissants.

1kg blueberries

Finely grated zest and juice of 2 large limes

3 tbsp water

600g jam sugar with added pectin

15g unsalted butter (optional)

Add half the blueberries to a preserving pan and roughly crush with a potato masher, then stir in the lime zest and juice and the water. Bring just to the boil then cook, uncovered, over a low heat for 5 minutes, stirring and crushing with the potato masher, until the berries are soft and have released lots of juice.

Stir in the sugar, then add the remaining blueberries. Cook over a low heat, stirring from time to time, until the sugar has completely dissolved.

Bring to the boil and boil rapidly for about 5 minutes, stirring from time to time, until setting point is reached. Take the pan off the heat and stir in the butter to disperse any remaining scum, if needed.

Ladle the hot jam into warmed sterilised jars right to the top, then screw on lids or cover with waxed discs and cellophane tops secured with elastic bands. Leave to cool, then label and date. Store in the fridge for up to one month.

Reduced-sugar strawberry and rhubarb jam

Rather than cooking the fruit in water first, macerating it with sugar and lemon juice will help to keep the colour of the finished jam bright. Rhubarb can react with some metals. If you have an old preserving pan, chances are it will be aluminium, which, depending on its finish, could give the jam a metallic taste. Use a stainless steel or non-stick coated aluminium preserving pan, stock pot or pasta pan. This jam thickens quickly once boiling starts, so stir frequently with a wooden spoon and begin checking for set after 5 minutes.

800g trimmed rhubarb, thinly sliced
400g strawberries, hulled and
    quartered

600g jam sugar with added pectin
Juice of ½ lemon
15g unsalted butter (optional)

Add the rhubarb and strawberries to a large china or glass dish, pour over the sugar and lemon juice, and stir together. Cover and leave for 4 hours or preferably overnight in the kitchen.

Tip the fruit and liquid into a preserving pan, using a flexible spatula to scrape out every last bit of sugar. Cook over a low heat, stirring from time to time, until the sugar has completely dissolved.

Bring to the boil and boil rapidly for 5–10 minutes, stirring from time to time, until setting point is reached.

Take the pan off the heat and stir in the butter to disperse any remaining scum, if needed. If there are any larger pieces of fruit, lightly crush with a potato masher. Ladle the hot jam into warmed sterilised jars right to the top, then screw on lids or cover with waxed discs and cellophane tops secured with elastic bands. Leave to cool, then label and date. Store in the fridge for up to 1 month.

Rhubarb

At Acorn Bank in Cumbria there is a large walled kitchen garden and a separate herb garden renowned for having the National Trust's most extensive collection of medicinal and culinary plants. Rhubarb appears in both. In the kitchen garden it is grown to supply the café and it is included in the herb garden because of its history of medicinal use. At Dyffryn Gardens in the Vale of Glamorgan harvesting volunteers deliver early forced rhubarb, and later the main crop, to the café twice a week to be used in the dishes served there.

Rhubarb is a prolific plant that is part of the buckwheat family. Its large structural leaves and coloured stems look just as good in a homely cottage garden as in a more modern minimal garden. To pick, twist the rhubarb stem rather than using a knife and trim off the leaves before weighing. Never eat the leaves as the high levels of oxalic acid makes them poisonous; add them to the compost instead.

English nurseryman Joseph Myatt pioneered the production of dessert rhubarb; he grew the variety 'Victoria' to honour Queen Victoria's accession to the throne in 1837 and this remains a popular variety.

Early or forced rhubarb comes into the shops from December to early March. These tender delicate pink stems are grown in large forcing sheds in the Rhubarb Triangle in West Yorkshire, and picked by candlelight. While large estate gardens would bring on rhubarb under beautiful pottery domes, most gardeners improvise with an upturned bucket. The main field crop makes the best jam and this is available from April to September. As the season nears the end, so the stems become thicker and more green than red.

Jellies

Making jelly

Unlike jam, fruit jellies are completely smooth. The secret to a good jelly is its clarity: it should be crystal clear. The key to achieving this is to leave the fruit mixture to drip through a jelly bag for several hours or overnight. Resist the urge to squeeze the jelly bag to get the maximum juice, or the finished jelly will be cloudy.

Skimming is also important for a clear jelly. While the liquid is boiling the movement of the rolling boil pushes the scum to the edges of the pan; a draining spoon with small holes will lift off the scum and allow the jelly to drip back into the pan. Try to keep skimming to a minimum, just once or twice during cooking. Some fruit mixtures will produce more scum and it can spoil the look of the finished preserve. While purists may disapprove, if skimming alone isn't working, you can add a tiny knob of butter, off the heat. Pot the jelly while hot as it will thicken quickly as it cools.

Scalding a jelly bag sterilises it before use. Put the jelly bag into a bowl and cover with boiling water. Leave for 5 minutes then drain well and hang from a frame, upturned stool or the handle of an overhead kitchen cupboard with a bowl or wide-necked jug set underneath to catch the juices. Choose a place where the jelly can drip undisturbed for several hours. After use, scoop out the fruit pulp and discard, rinse the jelly bag with plenty of hot water and leave to dry; don't be tempted to wash with detergent in the washing machine. Buy jelly bags from cookshops, department stores or online.

A sugar thermometer is a useful tool as you can see the temperature rise. Setting point is reached once the thermometer reads 105°C. Jelly sets quickly so get it in the jars as soon as possible.

Elderflower jelly

**There is nowhere to hide in this delicate pale yellow jelly, so it's
important to skim thoroughly and to use a good jelly bag.**

12 large open elderflower heads
Pared zest and juice of 1 lemon
1.5 litres water
1.5kg jam sugar with added pectin

Shake the elderflowers to dislodge any bugs, then add to a large glass
or china bowl with the pared lemon zest and water. Cover with a tea
towel or lid and leave in a cold place for 48 hours, ideally in the fridge.

Soak a square of muslin or clean linen tea towel in a bowl of boiling
water for a few minutes to sterilise it, then drain well and use to line
a large sieve set over the preserving pan. Pour the water, elderflowers
and lemon into the lined sieve. Squeeze out the juice, discard the
soaked flowers and lemon zest then bring to the boil.

Add the sugar and lemon juice to the pan and cook over a low heat,
stirring from time to time, until the sugar has completely dissolved.
Bring to the boil and boil rapidly for 10–15 minutes, stirring from
time to time, until setting point is reached. Skim off any scum from
around the edges of the pan once or twice with a draining spoon as
the liquid boils.

Turn off the heat and ladle the hot jelly into warmed sterilised jars
right to the top, then screw on lids or cover with waxed discs and
cellophane tops secured with elastic bands. Leave to cool, then label
and date. Store in a cool place.

Elderberry and orange jelly

Pot this fast-setting jelly straight away for a mirror-like finish.

450g elderberries (about 18–20 heads, stripped weight)
900g (about 4) cooking apples, washed and roughly chopped (no need to peel or core)
Pared zest and juice of 1 large orange, and squeezed orange shells, cut into large chunks
700ml water
5cm piece of cinnamon stick, halved
About 800g preserving sugar

Add the elderberries, cooking apples, pared orange zest, orange juice and chopped orange to a preserving pan. Pour in the water and add the cinnamon stick. Bring to the boil, then cover and cook over a low heat for 30 minutes, stirring from time to time and breaking up the fruit until soft. Leave to cool slightly.

Scald a jelly bag with boiling water, drain well, then suspend over a frame set above a bowl or large jug. Ladle the fruit and liquid into the jelly bag and leave to drip for 4 hours or until the dripping stops. Discard the fruit pulp.

Measure the juice, pour back into the washed preserving pan and reheat. For every 600ml of juice measure out 450g of preserving sugar. You should have about 1 litre so will need about 800g of sugar.

Add the sugar to the pan and cook over a low heat, stirring from time to time, until the sugar has completely dissolved. Bring to the boil and boil rapidly for about 10 minutes, stirring and skimming as needed, until setting point is reached.

Pour the hot jelly into warmed sterilised jars right to the top then screw on lids or cover with waxed discs and cellophane tops secured with elastic bands. Leave to cool, then label and date. Store in a cool place.

Plum jelly

Jelly is a great way to use small plums as there is no fiddly stoning to do before cooking. Naturally sweet Victoria plums with their pink blush skins and soft yellow flesh make a pretty jelly and are in season in the second half of August.

1.4kg small plums, left whole
700ml water

About 900g preserving sugar

Add the plums and water to a preserving pan, bring to the boil then cover and cook over a low heat for 25–30 minutes until the fruit is soft. Stir from time to time and crush with the back of a wooden spoon. Leave to cool slightly.

Scald a jelly bag with boiling water, drain well, then suspend over a frame set above a bowl or large jug. Ladle the fruit and liquid into the jelly bag and leave to drip for 4 hours or until the dripping stops. Discard the fruit pulp.

Measure the juice, pour back into the washed preserving pan and reheat. For every 600ml of juice, measure out 450g of sugar. You should have about 1.2 litres so will need about 900g of sugar.

Add the sugar to the pan and cook over a low heat, stirring from time to time, until the sugar has completely dissolved. Bring to the boil and boil rapidly for 10–15 minutes, stirring from time to time and skimming as needed, until setting point is reached.

Pour the hot jelly into warmed sterilised jars right to the top, then screw on lids or cover with waxed discs and cellophane tops secured with elastic bands. Leave to cool, then label and date. Store in a cool place.

Rose petal jelly

This fragrant jelly captures the beauty of an English rose garden.
Pick the rose petals on a dry sunny day, from roses with a deep
perfume, ideally with a deep colour too. Shake the flowers gently to
remove any insects, then tear off the petals and snip off the white
point from the base of the petals if large. Lightly pack the petals
into a measuring jug, being careful not to bruise them.

To finish the jelly add more rose petals, with the white bases
snipped off. Leave whole if they are small or chop so that the jelly
is speckled with bursts of colour. Leave the jelly to stand before
potting so that the petals don't float to the top. If they do rise in the
jars, stir gently with a skewer. This jelly is delicious spooned on to
small pieces of toast or to add a floral touch to rice pudding.

600ml rose petals, plus 300ml to
    finish, left whole, sliced or chopped
700ml cold water
450g jam sugar with added pectin
2 tbsp freshly squeezed lemon juice

Add 600ml rose petals to a bowl, pour over the cold water then cover
with a saucer so that the petals stay beneath the level of the water.
Leave in a cool place to infuse for 4–6 hours.

Soak a square of muslin or clean tea towel in a bowl of boiling water
for a few minutes to sterilise it, then drain and use to line a sieve set
over a measuring jug. Strain the rose petals through the sieve: you
should have 600ml of rose-scented water; top up with extra water if
necessary.

Pour the rose water into a preserving pan, bring just to the boil, then add the sugar and lemon juice, and cook over a low heat, stirring from time to time, until the sugar has completely dissolved. Bring to the boil and boil rapidly for 7–10 minutes, stirring from time to time and skimming as needed, until setting point is reached.

Turn off the heat and add the remaining rose petals, gently turning in the hot jelly. Leave to stand for 10 minutes to thicken slightly.

Ladle the jelly into warmed sterilised jars right to the top, then screw on lids or cover with waxed discs and cellophane tops secured with elastic bands. Leave to cool, then label and date. Store in a cool place.

Redcurrant and rhubarb jelly

Use this jelly to sandwich mini sponge cakes or spoon onto scones; it is equally good with grilled mackerel or barbecued lamb.

750g redcurrants, removed from
   strings
750g trimmed rhubarb, sliced

750ml water
About 1kg preserving sugar

Add the redcurrants and rhubarb to a preserving pan, pour in the water and bring to the boil. Cover and cook over a low heat for 30 minutes, stirring from time, and breaking up the rhubarb with a wooden spoon, until all the fruit is soft.

Scald a jelly bag with boiling water, drain well, then suspend from a frame over a large measuring jug or bowl. Ladle the fruit and liquid into the jelly bag and leave to drip for 4 hours or until the dripping stops. Discard the fruit pulp.

Measure the juice, pour back into the washed preserving pan and reheat. For every 600ml of juice measure out 450g of preserving sugar. You should have about 1.2 litres of juice, so will need about 1kg of sugar.

Add the sugar to the pan and cook over a low heat, stirring from time to time, until the sugar has completely dissolved. Bring to the boil and boil for about 15 minutes, stirring from time to time and skimming as needed, until setting point is reached.

Ladle into warmed sterilised jars right to the top. Scoop out any scum using a small spoon: it will rise to the top while the jelly is hot. Screw on lids or cover with waxed discs and cellophane tops secured with elastic bands. Leave to cool, then label and date. Store in a cool dry place.

Sloe and blackberry jelly

The apple provides a background note to the stronger flavours here, as well as boosting pectin levels to aid the set.

225g sloes (no need to stone)
400g blackberries
750g Bramley cooking apples, quartered and diced (no need to core or peel)
850ml water
About 800g preserving sugar

Add the sloes, blackberries and apples to a preserving pan, pour in the water and bring to the boil. Cover and cook over a low heat for 25–30 minutes until the fruit is soft, stirring from time to time and crushing the fruit with a wooden spoon to release the juices and pectin.

Scald a jelly bag with boiling water, drain well, then suspend from a frame over a large measuring jug or bowl. Ladle the fruit and liquid into the jelly bag and leave to drip for 4 hours or until the dripping stops. Discard the fruit pulp.

Measure the juice, pour back into the washed preserving pan and reheat. For every 600ml of juice measure out 450g of preserving sugar. You should have about 1 litre so will need about 800g of sugar.

Add the sugar to the pan and cook over a low heat, stirring from time to time, until the sugar has completely dissolved. Bring to the boil and boil rapidly for 10–15 minutes, stirring from time to time and skimming as needed, until setting point is reached.

Ladle the hot jelly into warmed sterilised jars right to the top. Scoop out any scum using a small spoon: it will rise to the top while the jelly is hot. Screw on lids or cover with waxed discs and cellophane tops secured with elastic bands. Leave to cool, then label and date. Store in a cool place.

From orchards and hedgerows

Popular for some 200 years, the Bramley cooking apple can be found in the orchards of stately homes, farms and family gardens all over the country. Amazingly, every single Bramley apple originated from one tree in Nottinghamshire that is still growing, albeit slightly gnarled and fragile now. Rich in pectin, the Bramley apple can be used in jellies, jams, butters and cheeses or mixed with fruits that are low in pectin to boost setting.

Bramley apples combine well with blackberries. The blackberry season begins just as the first Bramley apples begin to fall from the trees. Windfalls are great to use in jellies as any bruised areas can be cut away, and you don't need to peel and core the apples because the fruit is strained. Blackberries have lots of little seeds, which some people don't like; making them into jelly removes all the seeds. If you don't find quite enough wild blackberries in one trip, then freeze them until you do have enough. Try to pick blackberries on a dry day as they can quickly go mouldy.

Elderberries are ready at about the same time as blackberries but are rarely picked. The elder tree can often be seen in hedgerows; its glossy dark berries look like tiny blackcurrants that hang in large clusters known as umbels. Ideally, take a walking stick with you so that you can hook the branches down to a reachable height and pick the berries more easily and don't forget to tuck a bag into your jacket pocket so that you can bring them home. Collect elderberries on a dry day: you don't want them to be dripping water, which will affect the weight when measuring out ingredients. Choose elderberries away from busy roads. The National Trust own some of the most beautiful woodland all over the countryside and supports foraging for abundant species of wild food in most of their places, so long as the foraging is safe and sustainable, and for personal use.

Although elderberries are a little too sharp to eat raw, they make great jelly. To get 450g elderberries you will need about 18–20 large umbels, but pick a few more just in case. When stripping the elderberries from their stems, wear an apron as their dark juice will stain your clothes. Strip the berries from the umbels using your fingertips; the ripe black berries will come away easily while the pale green underripe ones will stay put. If a few underripe berries slip into the bowl, pick out as many as you can, but don't worry about any few that remain.

If you like foraging for hedgerow foods, then you may also like to try rowan jelly. The berries come from the rowan tree and hang in clusters of reddy orange berries. Mix with Bramley apples to ensure a good set.

Sloe gin is the first thing that comes to mind when we think of sloes. They have a rather bitter taste and are best not eaten raw or cooked on their own, but when mixed with blackberries they make a deliciously dark jelly. The sloe, or blackthorn, is a common hedgerow plant, often used as windbreaks or hedging as its long sharp thorns make the hedge almost impenetrable to livestock. In spring it produces beautiful white flowers. Sloes are members of the plum family and look a little like a black olive with a waxy blue bloom. Choose ripe sloes as they will be juicer. If you see some fallen on the ground then you will know that those still on the bush will be ready. Sloes store well in the fridge, so if you don't find quite enough on your first walk, or don't have time to make the jelly immediately, you can keep them in the fridge or freezer.

From late May to mid-June look out for the creamy white blossom sprays, or umbels, of elderflowers. Gather the elderflowers when freshly open on a dry sunny day and pick blossoms away from busy roads. They have a delicate sweet fragrance and can be used to make cordial, elderflower 'champagne', jellies and syrups for sorbet or ice cream. They can also be dipped in a light tempura batter and deep fried. The wonderful fragrance does attract insects so make sure to turn the umbels upside down and gently shake out any bugs before use. The blossoms wilt quickly, so try to use them soon after picking. Choose a large china, glass or plastic bowl for soaking, as metal can taint the flavour of the finished syrup or jelly.

Blackberry and port jelly

This luxurious jelly is a treat spooned over a toasted crumpet. It can also be served as an accompaniment to roast pheasant, venison, duck, beef or lamb. Quantities are only for a small amount so that the port flavour really comes through.

900g blackberries
300ml water
150ml ruby port

About 550g jam sugar with added pectin

Add the blackberries, water and port to a pan. Bring to the boil then cover and cook over a low heat for 30 minutes, stirring from time to time and lightly breaking up the berries with a wooden spoon or a potato masher. Leave to cool slightly.

Scald a jelly bag with boiling water, drain well, then suspend from a frame over a large bowl or jug. Ladle the fruit and juice into the jelly bag and leave to drip for 4 hours or until the dripping stops. Discard the fruit pulp.

Measure the juice, pour back into the washed pan and bring to the boil. For every 600ml of juice measure out 450g of jam sugar. You should have about 700ml so will need about 550g of sugar.

Add the sugar to the pan and cook over a low heat, stirring from time to time, until the sugar has completely dissolved. Bring to the boil and boil rapidly for 5–10 minutes, stirring from time to time and skimming as needed, until setting point is reached.

Ladle into warmed sterilised jars right to the top, then screw on lids or cover with waxed discs and cellophane tops secured with elastic bands. Leave to cool, then label and date. Store in a cool place.

Apple and blackberry jelly

This apple and blackberry jelly is lovely with newly baked bread spread with unsalted butter. You could also serve it with roast lamb instead of the more traditional redcurrant jelly.

1.1kg (about 5) Bramley cooking
    apples, washed and roughly
    chopped (no need to peel or core)
300g blackberries
850ml water
About 800g preserving sugar

Add the apples, blackberries and water to a preserving pan, bring to the boil, then cover and cook over a low heat for 30 minutes until the fruit is soft. Stir the fruit from time to time and crush lightly with the back of a wooden spoon. Leave to cool slightly.

Scald a jelly bag with boiling water, drain well, then suspend over a frame set above a bowl or large jug. Ladle the fruit and liquid into the jelly bag and leave to drip for 4 hours or until the dripping stops. Discard the fruit pulp.

Measure the juice, pour back into the washed preserving pan and reheat. For every 600ml of juice, measure out 450g of sugar. You should have about 1 litre so will need about 800g of sugar.

Add the sugar to the pan and cook over a low heat, stirring from time to time, until the sugar has completely dissolved. Bring to the boil and boil rapidly for about 10 minutes, stirring from time to time and skimming once or twice, until setting point is reached.

Pour the hot jelly into warmed sterilised jars right to the top, then screw on lids or cover with waxed discs and cellophane tops secured with elastic bands. Leave to cool, then label and date. Store in a cool place.

TIP The longer you leave the fruit mixture to drip the better. If left overnight it may make the difference of an extra 150ml of liquid or almost another jar of jelly. If you have wasps buzzing around the kitchen as the jelly drips, then wrap a tea towel around the frame holding the jelly bag and secure with laundry pegs so that they can't dive-bomb into the liquid.

Raspberry and lavender jelly

It's easy to imagine this elegant pink jelly in a pretty crystal glass container set among pedestal dishes of scones and delicate cucumber sandwiches. Perhaps just the kind of preserve that Edwardian socialite Mrs Margaret Greville would have served in her beautiful Tea Room at one of her weekend parties at Polesden Lacey in Surrey.

Adding just a few lavender heads to the raspberries and apples as they cook gives a gentle perfume. A little lavender goes a long way, so taste the strained juice once the sugar has dissolved. If you would like to add a little more, then tie one or two extra flower heads in muslin and add while the jelly is bought to setting point. Discard before potting.

500g raspberries
900g (about 4) Bramley cooking
   apples, washed and roughly
   chopped (no need to core or peel)

700ml water
3 large fresh or dried lavender flowers
About 800g preserving sugar

Add the raspberries, apples and water to a preserving pan, then add the lavender flowers. Bring to the boil then cook over a low heat for 25–30 minutes until the fruit is soft. Stir from time to time and crush the fruit lightly with the back of a wooden spoon. Leave to cool slightly.

Scald a jelly bag with boiling water, drain well, then suspend over a frame set above a bowl or large jug. Ladle the fruit and liquid into the jelly bag and leave to drip for 4 hours or until the dripping stops. Discard the fruit pulp.

Measure the juice, pour back into the washed preserving pan and reheat. For every 600ml of juice, measure out 450g of sugar. You should have about 1 litre so will need about 800g of sugar.

Add the sugar to the pan and cook over a low heat, stirring from time to time, until the sugar has completely dissolved. Bring to the boil and boil rapidly for 10–15 minutes, stirring from time to time and skimming as needed, until setting point is reached.

Pour the hot jelly into warmed sterilised jars right to the top, then screw on lids or cover with waxed discs and cellophane tops secured with elastic bands. Leave to cool, then label and date. Store in a cool place.

TIP Once the jelly has been potted and covered, you may like to tie a few stems of dried lavender around the top of each jar with a fine ribbon.

Blackcurrant jelly

**This tangy jelly has a surprise ingredient – beetroot. Its natural
sweetness will help to eke out the last of the blackcurrant crop.**

1kg blackcurrants (no need to top
 and tail)
400g (about 5–6 small) beetroot
 (trimmed weight), scrubbed
 and diced

1 litre water
About 900g preserving sugar

Add the blackcurrants and beetroot to a preserving pan, pour in the
water and bring to the boil. Cover and cook over a low heat for
45–60 minutes, stirring from time to time and roughly mashing the
beetroot with a potato masher once or twice, until the blackcurrants
and beetroot are soft. Leave to cool slightly.

Scald a jelly bag with boiling water, drain well, then suspend from a
frame over a large measuring jug or bowl. Ladle in the fruit mixture
and liquid and leave to drip for 4 hours or until the mixture stops
dripping. Discard the fruit and beetroot pulp.

Measure the liquid, pour back into the washed preserving pan and
reheat. For every 600ml of liquid measure out 450g of preserving sugar.
You should have about 1.2 litres so will need about 900g of sugar.

Pour the sugar into the pan and cook over a low heat, stirring from
time to time, until the sugar has completely dissolved. Bring to the
boil and boil rapidly for 10–15 minutes, stirring from time to time and
skimming as needed, until setting point is reached.

Pour into warmed sterilised jars right to the top, then screw on lids
or cover with waxed discs and cellophane tops secured with elastic
bands. Leave to cool, then label and date. Store in a cool place.

Fruit curds, butters and cheeses

Making fruit curds

Unlike other preserves, fruit curds need to be cooked gently. If you don't have a double boiler or double saucepan, improvise with a heatproof mixing bowl set over a saucepan of gently simmering water so that the eggs gently cook without curdling.

Unsalted butter is a must: you want the richness and silkiness of the butter but definitely not a salty taste.

Straining the eggs is important to prevent any strings of egg in the finished curd.

Fruit curds should have the texture of softly whipped cream and should coat the back of a wooden spoon when they are ready. The curd will thicken slightly as it cools. Make sure there are no air pockets when pouring the curd into the jars. To disperse air pockets, run a skewer through the preserve.

As these preserves are made with eggs, they must be kept in the fridge, whether sealed or opened.

Fruit curds make great Christmas gifts. Decorate the lids with circles of brown paper, baking paper or Christmas paper, and tie in place with raffia or ribbon, adding a bay leaf or two along with a gift label recommending that the preserve is kept in the fridge.

Lemon curd with lemon thyme

Here the favourite lemon curd is given a subtle twist of thyme.

Finely grated zest and juice of 3 large
  lemons
115g unsalted butter, diced

400g caster sugar
1 tbsp fresh lemon thyme leaves
4 eggs, beaten

Half fill a saucepan with water and set a heatproof mixing bowl on top so that the water doesn't touch the base of the bowl or use a double boiler if you have one. Add the lemon zest and juice to the bowl, then add the butter, sugar and thyme leaves. Heat, stirring from time to time, until the butter has melted and the sugar has begun to dissolve.

Strain the eggs through a sieve into the lemon mixture and stir well. Cook for 30–40 minutes, stirring from time to time, until thickened.

Ladle the hot curd into warmed sterilised jars, add a waxed disc and a cellophane cover and secure with an elastic band. Leave to cool, then label and date. Store in the fridge and eat within 2 weeks.

VARIATIONS For purists, you can leave out the thyme. Or for a romantic option, add the pulp and seeds from 3 halved passion fruit when stirring in the strained eggs.

If you have a slow cooker, you might like to cook the curd in this instead. Warm the butter, sugar, fruit zest and juice in a small saucepan until the butter has melted and the sugar dissolved, then transfer to a heatproof basin that will fit inside your slow cooker pot. Strain the eggs into the fruit mix and stir together. Pour hot water from the kettle to come halfway up the sides of the basin, then cover with the slow cooker lid and cook for 3–4 hours on low, stirring once, and then again at the end, until very thick. Pot as above.

Gooseberry curd

Acidic fruits such as gooseberries work well in fruit curds but they must be cooked and sieved first to remove their tiny seeds. When cooked, gooseberries lose a little of their colour. You can stir in a drop or two of green food colouring to enhance the colour (use red food colouring if you have red gooseberries), but this is optional and best stirred into the thickened curd just before potting.

300g gooseberries, topped and tailed
Finely grated zest and juice of
   1 lemon
4 tbsp water

115g unsalted butter, diced
400g caster sugar
4 eggs, beaten

Add the gooseberries, lemon zest and juice and water to a saucepan, cover and cook over a low heat for about 15 minutes until the fruit is soft. Leave to cool slightly.

Purée the gooseberries and lemony juices in a food processor or blender, then press through a sieve set over a bowl and discard the seeds.

Set a heatproof mixing bowl over a saucepan of simmering water so that the water doesn't touch the base of the bowl, or transfer the gooseberry purée to a double boiler if you have one. Add the butter and sugar and heat, stirring from time to time, until the butter has melted and the sugar has begun to dissolve.

Strain the eggs through a sieve into the gooseberry mix and stir well. Cook for 40–50 minutes, stirring from time to time, until the curd has thickened.

Ladle the hot curd into warmed sterilised jars, add a waxed disc and a cellophane cover and secure with an elastic band. Leave to cool, then label and date. Store in the fridge and eat within 2 weeks.

VARIATION The same weight of prepared cooking apples can be used instead of gooseberries, adding a little freshly grated ginger or chopped stem ginger (drained of its syrup) for extra flavour. Or try with cooked cranberries – frozen ones work fine – with a little orange juice, or a mix of raspberries and red grapefruit juice.

Lemon and elderflower curd

Look out for fresh clusters of creamy white elderflower blossom in the hedgerows towards the end of May and capture their delicate perfume in an easy-to-make syrup. The season is short so make double the quantity and freeze in an ice cube tray.

FOR THE ELDERFLOWER SYRUP
115g caster sugar
200ml water
Pared zest and juice of 1 lemon
6 elderflower heads

FOR THE LEMON CURD
Finely grated zest and juice of
  1 lemon
115g unsalted butter, diced
225g caster sugar
4 eggs, beaten
1 elderflower head (optional)

To make the syrup, add the sugar and water to a small saucepan and heat gently, stirring from time to time, until the sugar has dissolved. Bring to the boil and boil for 1 minute, then take off the heat and leave until warm.

Add the pared lemon zest and juice to the syrup and stir well. Shake the elderflower heads to remove any tiny insects then put into a sealable glass, plastic or ceramic container. Pour over the warm syrup and press the elderflowers to submerge them in the syrup. Cover and leave until cold, then place in the fridge overnight. Shake the container whenever you go to the fridge to encourage the elderflower perfume to infuse the syrup.

Next day, half fill a saucepan with water and set a heatproof mixing bowl on top so that the water doesn't touch the base of the bowl, or use a double boiler if you have one. Add the lemon zest and juice, butter and sugar to the bowl, and heat until the butter has melted.

Meanwhile, rinse a square of muslin with boiling water, wring out and line a sieve with it. Set the sieve over a jug and pour in the elderflower syrup. Draw up the corners of the muslin and squeeze out the remaining juice, then discard the contents of the muslin.

Stir the syrup into the butter mixture, then strain the eggs through the sieve into the bowl and stir until smooth. Pick off the flowers from the remaining elderflower head, if using, and stir again, then cook for 40–50 minutes, stirring from time to time, until the curd has thickened.

Ladle the hot curd into warmed sterilised jars, add a waxed disc and a cellophane cover and secure with an elastic band. Leave to cool, then label and date. Store in the fridge and eat within 2 weeks.

Orange and bay curd

If you have a bay tree, you'll know that the leaves are just as good in the depths of winter as in the summer months. You need fresh bay leaves for this curd so pick up a pack from your local supermarket if necessary.

Grated zest and juice of 2 large
   oranges
Juice of ½ lemon
115g unsalted butter, diced

340g caster sugar
2 fresh bay leaves
4 eggs, beaten

Half fill a saucepan with water and set a heatproof mixing bowl on top so that the water doesn't touch the base of the bowl, or use a double boiler if you have one. Measure out the orange juice and add 170ml to the bowl along with the orange zest and lemon juice.

Add the butter, sugar and bay leaves, and heat, stirring from time to time, until the butter has melted and the sugar has begun to dissolve.

Strain the eggs through a sieve into the orange mixture and stir well. Cook for 40–50 minutes, stirring from time to time, until the curd has thickened.

Discard the bay leaves from the curd, or take them out and add one to each jar if preferred. Ladle the hot curd into warmed sterilised jars, add a waxed disc and a cellophane cover and secure with an elastic band. Leave to cool, then label and date. Store in the fridge and eat within 2 weeks.

VARIATION St Clements curd: Instead of 2 large oranges use the zest and juice of 1 medium orange and 2 lemons. Leave out the bay leaves.

Blackberry curd

This deeply coloured curd has a tangy blackberry flavour. It is lovely to pick your own blackberries when out walking but if you don't have time, shop-bought fresh or frozen blackberries are fine.

340g blackberries
2 tbsp water
115g unsalted butter, diced

340g caster sugar
4 eggs, beaten

Add the blackberries and water to a food processor or blender and purée. Press the purée through a sieve set over a heatproof bowl and discard the seeds.

Half fill a saucepan with water and set the bowl on top so that the water doesn't touch the base of the bowl, or transfer the purée to a double boiler if you have one. Add the butter and heat until melted, then add the sugar and the blackberry purée and mix together.

Strain the eggs through a sieve into the blackberry mix and stir well. Cook for 40–50 minutes, stirring from time to time, until the curd has thickened.

Ladle the hot curd into warmed sterilised jars, add a waxed disc and a cellophane cover and secure with an elastic band. Leave to cool, then label and date. Store in the fridge and eat within 2 weeks.

VARIATION Stir in the finely grated zest of an orange, a little ground cinnamon or some finely chopped fresh mint when mixing in the eggs.

Making fruit butters

Fruit butters have a soft smooth texture, delicious spread over good bread or used to fill a walnut sponge cake or lemon-flavoured Swiss roll. Or serve them instead of chutney or pickle with cold meats, or as part of a ploughman's lunch with mature cheddar cheese.

First, cook the fruit with liquid to make a purée, then weigh the purée to calculate how much sugar you will need. Allow half sugar to fruit purée for naturally sweet fruits or up to three quarters sugar to fruit purée if the fruit is a little sharper. You will need 225–340g of sugar to each 450g of fruit purée.

To cook the purée with the sugar you will need a heavy-based preserving pan. Stir regularly and keep an eye on the mixture, as it can easily catch and burn. Stir more frequently towards the end of cooking time as the mixture thickens and the bubbles become larger and slower. A knob of unsalted butter adds richness and a silky smoothness. Use a flexible spatula to get the last of the fruit butter out of the pan: you'll be surprised at how much clings to the side of the pan.

Fruit butters are easy to make and once you have made one you will be able to adapt the basic recipe and try with different fruits. For fruits that have a high water content, reduce the amount of liquid slightly. As the purée is weighed in order to calculate the amount of sugar needed, this gives plenty of room to experiment. Fresh apricots, blackcurrants, crab apples, cranberries, medlars and plums make good fruit butters. You might also like to try adding spices such as cardamom, cinnamon or ginger, or tangy citrus fruit zest and juice.

Windfall apple and apricot butter

This is a great way to use up windfall apples with a pack of dried apricots from the cupboard. You don't need to core or peel the apples, just wash them, cut away any bruising, then roughly chop.

175g ready-to-eat dried apricots
150ml boiling water
1kg windfall Bramley cooking apples,
    any bruised parts cut out, roughly
    chopped (no need to peel or core)

200ml water
Grated zest and juice of 1 lemon
About 500g granulated sugar
25g unsalted butter

Add the apricots to a bowl and cover with the boiling water; set aside while you cook the apples.

Add the apples and water to a preserving pan and bring to the boil. Cover and simmer for 20–25 minutes, stirring from time to time and breaking up the apples with a wooden spoon until they are soft. Leave to cool slightly. Press the mixture through a wide-meshed sieve set over a bowl. Discard the skins and pips.

Tip the soaked apricots and water into a food processor or blender with the lemon zest and juice, and blend until smooth. Add the apple pulp and blend again briefly.

Weigh the purée, then pour back into the washed preserving pan and reheat. For every 450g of purée weigh out 225g of sugar. You should have about 1kg of purée so will need about 500g of sugar.

Add the sugar to the pan and cook over a low heat, stirring from time to time, until the sugar has completely dissolved. Increase the heat slightly and continue to cook for about 25 minutes, stirring from time to time, until the mixture has thickened and darkened slightly. Stir more frequently towards the end of cooking as the mixture thickens.

When ready, the fruit butter will fall in large clumps from the wooden spoon.

Take off the heat and stir in the butter. Ladle the hot fruit butter into warmed sterilised jars right to the top, then draw a skewer or fine fork through the preserve to disperse any air bubbles. Clip or screw on lids, or cover the tops with waxed discs and cellophane tops secured with elastic bands. Leave to cool, then label and date. Store in a cool place.

TIP If you haven't got quite enough to fill the third jar, cover the surface with a waxed disc and then fill the gap with a piece of crumpled baking paper. Store in the fridge and use this jar first.

Cidered apple butter

Using cider instead of water enhances the apple flavour in this autumnal fruit butter.

1.5kg Bramley cooking apples, roughly chopped (no need to peel or core)

500ml dry cider
About 1kg preserving sugar
About 40g unsalted butter

Add the apples to a preserving pan, pour in the cider and bring to the boil. Cover and simmer for 25–30 minutes, stirring the fruit from time to time, until soft. Leave to cool. Press the mixture through a wide-meshed sieve set over a bowl. Discard the skin and pips. Purée the fruit pulp in a food processor or blender until smooth.

Weigh the purée, then pour back into the washed preserving pan and reheat. For every 450g of purée weigh out 340g of sugar. You should have about 1.4kg of purée so will need about 1kg of sugar.

Add the sugar to the pan and cook over a low heat, stirring from time to time, until the sugar has completely dissolved. Increase the heat slightly and continue to cook for about 45 minutes, stirring from time to time, until the mixture has thickened and darkened slightly. Stir more frequently as the mixture thickens. When ready, the fruit butter will fall in large clumps from the wooden spoon.

Take off the heat and stir in the butter, allowing 15g for every 450g of fruit purée. Ladle the hot mixture into warmed sterilised jars right to the top, then draw a skewer or fine fork through the preserve to disperse any air bubbles. Clip or screw on lids, or cover with waxed discs and cellophane tops secured with elastic bands. Leave to cool, then label and date. Store in a cool place for up to 1 month.

Making fruit cheeses

Fruit cheeses may have got their name because they were often eaten in place of a cheese course, or it may be because they set firm and can be sliced like cheese.

Fruit cheeses take a while to cook, but they need only minimal attention, just occasionally stirring so that the mixture doesn't stick. Aim to cook the cheese while you are ironing or doing some other kitchen chore so that you can keep an eye on the pan as it quietly bubbles away. This is not the kind of recipe you can leave unattended.

First you need to cook the fruit with water until soft, then press it through a sieve to remove all the pips, peel, etc to leave a smooth purée. A potato masher can speed things up, or use a mouli or rotary grater fitted with a small to medium disc.

A heavy-based preserving pan is essential for the next stage. Cook the purée with the sugar over a medium heat, stirring from time to time, until the mixture thickens. Be patient! This is not a process you can hurry: the heat needs to be just high enough for the mixture to bubble gently so that excess liquid is driven off, but not so high that it burns on the base of the pan. As the mixture thickens, so the size of the bubbles will increase, giving you a clue that you are nearly there. You know when the cheese is ready by its thickness and not by the temperature or saucer test. It will be so thick that you will be able to see the base of the pan momentarily as you drag the wooden spoon through the purée. Once the cheese gets as thick as this, you will need to stir the mixture constantly so that it doesn't catch and spoil the colour and flavour of the cheese.

It is perfectly fine to use granulated sugar. The fruit mixture is puréed so the clarity of this preserve is not so important.

When ready, spoon the hot mixture into shallow wide-necked jars, ideally with straight sides that have been lightly oiled.

Traditionally fruit cheeses would be set in a wooden mould with a layer of liquid paraffin on top to seal it. Clip-top (Le Parfait-style) glass jars are a better option for the modern cook, or freezer-to-oven style individual glass dishes with clip-on plastic lids. If you don't have quite enough to fill the jar, then cover the surface with baking paper and fold it back over itself to fill the gap. As the cheese cools, moisture will gather under the lid then drip onto the paper rather than the cheese, which could cause mould to form.

When ready to serve, run a knife around the edge, then invert the jar onto a plate and jerk to release. Slice and enjoy with strong cheese such as Stilton or mature cheddar, or a crumbly, slightly acidic Wensleydale, or cooked meats.

Gingered pear and apple cheese

Ideally you want just-ripe pears, full of flavour, for this recipe.

700g just-ripe pears, roughly chopped
(no need to peel or core)
700g Bramley cooking apples, roughly
chopped (no need to peel or core)
100g fresh ginger, finely chopped (no
need to peel)

425ml water
About 1.2kg granulated sugar
15g unsalted butter
Sunflower or vegetable oil for greasing

Add the pears, apples, ginger and water to a preserving pan and bring
to the boil. Cover and simmer for about 30 minutes, stirring from time
to time and breaking up the fruit with a wooden spoon, until very soft.

Press the fruit through a wide-meshed sieve set over a large bowl to
remove the skins and pips, then purée the pulp in batches in a food
processor or blender until smooth. Weigh the fruit purée, then return
to the washed preserving pan and reheat. For every 450g of purée add
450g of sugar to the pan and cook over a low heat, stirring from time
to time, until the sugar has completely dissolved.

Increase the heat slightly and cook for 45–60 minutes, stirring from
time to time, until the mixture begins to thicken and darken slightly.
Stir more frequently towards the end of cooking time, lowering the
heat if needed. The cheese is ready when you draw a wooden spoon
through the mixture and you can see the base of the pan briefly.

Take the pan off the heat and stir in the butter. Brush the inside of
two warmed sterilised jars with a little oil, then ladle in the hot cheese
right to the top. Draw a skewer through the jars to disperse any air
bubbles. Screw or clip the lids in place. Leave to cool, then label and
date. Store in a cool place.

Quince cheese

Serve this cheese with goats' cheese, manchego or strong cheddar.

1.8kg quinces, soft down rubbed from the skins, rinsed and roughly chopped
2 litres water

About 1.4kg granulated sugar
15g unsalted butter (optional)
Sunflower or vegetable oil for greasing

Add the quinces and water to a preserving pan, bring to the boil, then cover and simmer for 1 hour, stirring from time to time and breaking up the fruit with a wooden spoon, until the quinces are very soft.

Press the fruit mixture through a wide-meshed sieve set over a large bowl to remove the skin and pips, then purée the fruit pulp in a food processor or blender until smooth.

Weigh the fruit purée, then return to the washed preserving pan and reheat. For every 450g of purée add 450g of sugar to the pan and cook over a low heat, stirring from time to time, until the sugar has completely dissolved.

Increase the heat slightly and cook for 45–60 minutes, stirring from time to time, until the mixture begins to thicken and darken slightly. Stir more frequently towards the end of cooking, lowering the heat if needed. The cheese is ready when you draw the wooden spoon through the mixture and you can see the base of the pan briefly.

Stir in the butter to disperse any scum, if needed. Brush the inside of two warmed sterilised jars with a little oil, then ladle in the hot cheese right to the top. Draw a skewer through the jars to disperse any air bubbles. Screw or clip the lids in place. Leave to cool, then label and date. Store in a cool place.

Quinces

The ancient Greeks associated the quince with love and fertility and offered the fruit as a wedding gift. Greek brides were known to bite into a quince to perfume their first kiss before entering the bridal chamber. In Greek myth, the golden apples of the Hesperides, given to Aphrodite by Paris of Troy, were probably quinces too.

Most varieties of quince are too hard and too astringent to be eaten raw. Rich in pectin, quinces were often cooked with honey and water and then set in wooden moulds. This fragrant preserve was sliced or cut into small squares and is said to have been given to Henry VIII. Known as *membrillo* in Spain, *marmelo* in Portugal and *marmelatta* in Italy, it is thought to be the forerunner to the marmalade we enjoy today.

By the sixteenth century quince trees were grown in British kitchen gardens and orchards. The first recorded British recipe for a quince preserve called Red Marmelett dates from 1610.

Quinces are available in late autumn. They look like a large, knobbly yellow pear with a fuzzy skin. If cooking quinces unpeeled, you will need to rub off the downy fluff with a tea towel. When cut they have a pale, almost pear-coloured flesh with a taste like an aromatic, lemony pear. Although the flesh is white, when cooked the tannins break down, releasing anthocyanin, a natural pigment that gives quince cheese its deep russet colour.

Damson cheese

Damson trees can be found in many old rural gardens and in the hedgerows surrounding fields or woodland. The mature trees in the orchard at Brockhampton Estate, Herefordshire, produce delicious fruit for jams and damson gin.

1.4kg damsons or other small plums (no need to stone or halve)
425ml water

About 1.4kg granulated sugar
15g unsalted butter (optional)
Sunflower or vegetable oil for greasing

Add the plums and water to a preserving pan and bring to the boil. Cover and simmer for 20–25 minutes, stirring from time to time and breaking up the fruit with a potato masher, until very soft. Discard the stones.

Weigh the fruit purée, then return to the washed preserving pan and reheat. For every 450g of purée add 450g of sugar to the pan. Cook over a low heat, stirring from time to time, until the sugar has dissolved.

Increase the heat slightly and cook for 45–60 minutes, stirring from time to time, until the mixture thickens and darkens slightly. Stir more frequently towards the end of cooking time, lowering the heat if needed. The cheese is ready when you can draw a wooden spoon through the mixture and see the base of the pan briefly.

Take off the heat and stir in the butter to disperse any remaining scum, if needed. Brush the inside of two warmed sterilised wide-necked jars with a little oil, then ladle in the hot cheese right to the top. Draw a skewer through the mixture to disperse any air bubbles. Screw or clip the lids in place. Leave to cool, then label and date. Store in a cool place.

VARIATION Mulberries or a half-and-half mix of mulberries and cooking apples can be made into a deep red fruit cheese in the same way.

Marmalade

Seville orange marmalade

Seville orange marmalade is the most traditional of all British marmalade recipes. It is made from the slightly knobbly Spanish Seville oranges, which have a slightly thicker layer of bitter pith than other oranges and are most suited to cooking. Look out for them in the shops in early January for about six weeks. Their season is short, so if you don't have time to make marmalade when you see them, pop them in the freezer then defrost and use later. If using defrosted fruit, remember to add an extra 10% more than the recipe states so that the setting is not affected.

As the pith of Seville oranges is so tough, it is easier to cook the oranges whole and then to shred the peel and pith once they have been softened.

1kg (about 12–13 small) Seville oranges, washed
1.2 litres boiling water

Juice of 1 lemon
2kg granulated sugar, warmed
15g unsalted butter (optional)

Put the whole oranges into a saucepan so that they fit tightly together, pour over the water and bring to the boil. Cover and simmer for 2–2¼ hours until the oranges are soft and can be pierced easily with a skewer. Lift the oranges out of the water, reserving the cooking liquid (you should have about 700ml, top up with a little extra water if needed), and leave to cool.

Thinly slice the oranges, discarding any pips and green calyx, and add the oranges to a preserving pan with the reserved cooking liquid and lemon juice. Bring to the boil then stir in the warmed sugar. Cook over a low heat, stirring from time to time, until the sugar has completely dissolved. Bring to the boil and boil rapidly for 15–20 minutes, stirring from time to time, until setting point is reached.

Take the pan off the heat and stir in the butter to disperse any scum, if needed. Ladle the hot marmalade into warmed sterilised jars right to the top, then screw on lids or cover with waxed discs and cellophane tops secured with elastic bands. Leave to cool, then label and date. Store in a cool place.

Marmalade

'Fancy her knowing I like marmalade,' said Paddington.

(from *A bear called Paddington* by Michael Bond)

The polite little bear from darkest Peru is easily recognisable from his blue duffel coat and battered red felt hat. He often tucked a marmalade sandwich in his hat in case of emergency.

He is not the only one to love marmalade: the Queen is known to enjoy marmalade for breakfast, while Sir Edmund Hilary took a jar up Everest in 1953. Winston Churchill was also a fan and insisted that boats carrying oranges got through during the war to 'boost morale'.

One of the earliest recipes for orange marmalade is found in Madam Eliza Cholmondeley's handwritten recipe book, dated around 1677. The peel and pith were soaked in water for 3–4 days, then boiled until soft, and shredded before being cooked with the fruit flesh and juice and sugar until thick and 'it comes clean from the base of the skillet'. It was more like the quince cheeses and solid fruit pastes that were popular at the time. A later recipe by Mary Kettilby that appeared in her book 'A Collection of Above Three Hundred Receipts in Cookery, Physick and Surgery', published around 1714, also uses whole oranges and sugar plus lemon juice and says to 'boil it pretty fast until it will jelly'. This suggests it was closer to the marmalade we know today.

Queen Anne had one of Britain's first orangeries built at Kensington Palace in 1704 to house her collection of citrus fruits. At Hanbury Hall in Worcestershire, the eighteenth-century formal gardens have been painstakingly restored and include an orangery complete with citrus plants. Orangeries were built not just to protect citrus trees, peach trees and nectarine trees, but also as symbol of wealth and status. With the abolition of the glass tax in 1851 and improvements to glass production, their popularity was at its height during the

Victorian era. Stoves and pipes warmed the structures during the winter. The National Trust is the largest single owner of orangeries in the UK, including the 130-metre Long Range Glasshouse at Clumber Park in Nottinghamshire and those at Tyntesfield in North Somerset and Knole in Kent.

James Keiller of Dundee is credited with producing the first commercial brand of Seville orange marmalade. The story goes that in the late eighteenth century he bought a large quantity of oranges from a storm-damaged ship. His family owned a confectionery shop and his wife used the oranges to make marmalade containing chunks of peel. The company expanded rapidly and by the late nineteenth century Keiller's marmalade was enjoyed around the world.

Orange marmalade is by far the most popular type, but it can be made with any citrus fruits. Marmalade is lovely to make but there is no getting away from it, shredding oranges by hand can take ages. If you hope to make marmalade frequently, it may be worth investing in a good food processor with a citrus-squeezing attachment. Use this to make light work of squeezing the juice, then fit the metal slicing blade for shredding the peel and pith.

When cooking the fruit it is important to make sure that the shreds are tender, as they will not soften further once the sugar is added. To check if they are cooked enough, squeeze a shred between your finger and thumb – it should be easy to press.

As marmalade is made with citrus fruit and includes the pectin-rich but bitter pith, you will need to add more sugar to fruit than when making jam. Warm the sugar in a roasting tin in the oven set to 130°C alongside the jam jars as you sterilise them for 10–15 minutes. Warmed sugar, added to just cooked fruit rinds and juice, will dissolve much faster than when added cold. Make sure the sugar has completely dissolved before you increase the heat and boil to setting point; if it hasn't fully dissolved it may crystallise. You can use either granulated or preserving sugar.

Dark Oxford marmalade

Oxford marmalade was first made in 1874 by Sarah-Jane Cooper, the wife of Oxford shopkeeper Frank Cooper, and it soon became a popular brand. Captain Scott took a jar to Antarctica, which was later found buried in the ice.

Rather than Seville oranges, this version uses oranges that are available all year round, with the addition of lemon juice for a sharper Seville orange-style taste. Dark muscovado sugar gives a rich caramel flavour, but is balanced with white sugar so that the orange flavour is not hidden.

1kg (about 6) oranges, washed and halved	1.1kg granulated sugar
2 lemons, washed and halved	250g dark muscovado sugar
1.5 litres water	15g unsalted butter (optional)
	3–4 tsp black treacle (optional)

Squeeze the juice from the oranges and lemons, reserving the pips and shells. Tip the juice into a jug, cover and reserve in the fridge. Tie the pips in a square of muslin.

Cut the orange and lemon shells in half again then thinly slice using a large sharp knife or a food processor fitted with a thin slicer blade. Add to a large china or glass bowl, then add the water and the muslin bag of pips. Cover and leave at room temperature to soak for 4 hours or overnight.

Tip the soaked shreds, water and muslin bag into a preserving pan, add the reserved fruit juice and bring to the boil. Reduce the heat and simmer uncovered over a medium to low heat for 1½–2 hours, stirring from time to time, until the shreds are soft and the mixture has reduced by half to about 1.5 litres.

Squeeze the muslin bag between two wooden spoons held just above the pan so that the juice runs back into the pan. Discard the bag. Add both sugars to the pan and stir together, then cook over a low heat, stirring from time to time, until the sugars have completely dissolved.

Bring to the boil and boil rapidly for 15–20 minutes, stirring from time to time, until setting point is reached. Take the pan off the heat and stir in the butter to disperse any remaining scum, if needed. Stir in the treacle, if using. Ladle into warmed sterilised jars right to the top, then screw on lids or cover with waxed discs and cellophane tops secured with elastic bands. Leave to cool, then label and date. Store in a cool place.

Three-fruit marmalade

This easy, speedy marmalade can be made at any time of the year.

1 ruby grapefruit, washed
2 large oranges, washed
2 lemons, washed
1.5 litres water
1.8kg granulated sugar, warmed
15g unsalted butter (optional)

Cut each fruit into chunks and reserve the pips. Add the fruit to a food processor in batches and pulse until finely chopped. Transfer to a preserving pan with any juice left on the chopping board. Tie the pips in a square of muslin and add to the pan.

Pour the water into the pan and bring to the boil. Reduce the heat and simmer uncovered over a medium to low heat for about 1½ hours, stirring from time to time, until the peel is soft and the mixture has reduced by half to about 1.2 litres.

Lift the muslin bag into a ladle and hold above the pan; using a wooden spoon, press the bag so that the juices run back into the pan. Discard the bag. Pour in the sugar, stir well, then cook over a low heat, stirring from time to time, until the sugar has completely dissolved.

Bring to the boil and boil rapidly for 10–15 minutes, stirring from time to time, until setting point is reached. Take the pan off the heat and stir in the butter to disperse any remaining scum, if needed. Ladle into warmed sterilised jars right to the top, then screw on lids or cover with waxed discs and cellophane tops secured with elastic bands. Leave to cool, then label and date. Store in a cool place.

Frugal orange and apple marmalade

This recipe, dating from times of wartime rationing, makes the most of orange peel that would otherwise be discarded. Save any discarded peelings over the week in a plastic container in the fridge.

450g orange peel with pith (from 6–7 oranges), cut into thin strips
1.5 litres water
450g prepared weight of windfall

cooking apples, cored, peeled and diced, reserving the trimmings
1.4kg granulated sugar, warmed
15g unsalted butter (optional)

Add the orange shreds to a large china or glass dish and pour over the water. Cover and leave at room temperature to soak overnight.

The next day, tip the orange shreds and water into a preserving pan, bring to the boil, then simmer uncovered over a medium to low heat for 1½ hours, stirring from time to time, until the orange shreds have softened and the mixture has reduced down to about 1 litre.

Tie the apple peel, cores and pips in a square of muslin. Add to the preserving pan with the diced apple, cover and simmer for 30–40 minutes until the orange shreds and apples are soft. Stir from time to time and more frequently towards the end of cooking so that the apple doesn't stick to the base of the pan.

Lift the muslin bag of apple trimmings into a ladle and hold above the pan; using a wooden spoon, press the bag so that the pectin-rich juices run back into the pan. Discard the bag. Pour in the sugar, stir well, then cook over a low heat, stirring from time to time, until the sugar has completely dissolved.

Bring to the boil and boil rapidly for 15–20 minutes, stirring from time to time, until setting point is reached. Turn off the heat, stir in the butter to disperse any remaining scum, if needed, and leave to stand for 10 minutes.

Ladle the hot marmalade into warmed sterilised jars right to the top, then screw on lids or cover with waxed discs and cellophane tops secured with elastic bands. Leave to cool, then label and date. Store in a cool place.

VARIATION If you like ginger, add some finely grated fresh ginger when cooking the orange shreds.

Apricot and orange marmalade

Dried apricots boost the natural sweetness of this marmalade.

1kg (about 6–7 medium) oranges, washed and halved
2 lemons, washed, halved
1.5 litres water

250g dried apricots, chopped
1kg granulated sugar
225g demerara sugar
15g unsalted butter (optional)

Squeeze the juice from the citrus fruit and reserve along with the pips. Cut the orange peel and pith into fine strips and add to a large china or glass dish. Cut the lemon shells into chunky pieces and tie in a square of muslin with the pips; add to the orange peel. Pour over the water, cover the dish and leave at room temperature to soak overnight. Pour the fruit juice into a jug, cover and transfer to the fridge.

Next day, transfer the orange shreds, muslin bag and water to a preserving pan, bring to the boil, then simmer uncovered over a medium to low heat for 1½ hours, stirring occasionally. You should have about 1.5 litres at this stage, excluding the muslin bag. Add the reserved fruit juice and chopped apricots to the pan and simmer for 20–30 minutes, stirring occasionally, until the apricots and orange shreds are soft. Meanwhile, mix the sugars in a roasting tin and warm in the oven at 120°C for 15 minutes.

Lift the muslin bag into a ladle and hold above the pan; using a wooden spoon, press the bag so that the juices run back into the pan. Discard the bag. Stir in the warmed sugars and cook over a low heat, stirring from time to time, until the sugars have completely dissolved. Bring to the boil and boil rapidly for 15–20 minutes, stirring from time to time, until setting point is reached. Take the pan off the heat and stir in the butter to disperse any remaining scum, if needed. Ladle into warmed sterilised jars right to the top, then screw on lids or cover with waxed discs and cellophane tops secured with elastic bands. Leave to cool, then label and date. Store in a cool place.

Ruby grapefruit marmalade

Ruby grapefruit make a delicate pink marmalade with a tangy bittersweet flavour. Wash the skins well and don't forget to remove the tiny green calyx from the top.

3 ruby grapefruit, washed, quartered
1.5 litres water
Juice of 2 lemons
1.4kg granulated sugar, warmed
15g unsalted butter (optional)

Cut the peel and pith away from the grapefruit, put the skins to one side and tie the pips in a square of muslin.

Chop the fruit, including the membrane between the segments, in a food processor or with a large sharp knife on a chopping board set in a Swiss roll tin to catch the juices, then add to a preserving pan.

Finely slice the peel and pith, and add to the preserving pan with the muslin bag and the water, bring to the boil then simmer uncovered over a medium to low heat for 1½–2 hours, stirring from time to time, until the skins are softened and the mixture has reduced by half to just over 1.2 litres.

Lift the muslin bag into a ladle and hold above the pan; using a wooden spoon, press the bag so that the juices run back into the pan. Discard the bag. Stir in the lemon juice and sugar, and cook over a low heat, stirring from time to time, until the sugar has completely dissolved. Bring to the boil and boil rapidly for 15–20 minutes, stirring from time to time, until setting point is reached.

Take the pan off the heat and stir in the butter to disperse any remaining scum, if needed. Leave to stand for 10–15 minutes. Ladle into warmed sterilised jars right to the top, then screw on lids or cover with waxed discs and cellophane tops secured with elastic bands. Leave to cool, then label and date. Store in a cool place.

Caribbean pineapple marmalade

While pineapple may not seem an obvious choice for marmalade, its sweet juicy flesh is delicious when cooked with oranges, lemons and limes.

4 oranges, washed and halved
2 large limes, washed and halved
1 lemon, washed and halved
1.5 litres water

225g prepared weight fresh pineapple
    (half a medium pineapple),
    finely chopped
1.4kg granulated sugar, warmed
15g unsalted butter (optional)

Squeeze the juice from the oranges, limes and lemon, and add to a preserving pan. Reserve the pips and tie in muslin. Finely shred the squeezed fruit shells including the pith and peel using a large sharp knife or in a food processor.

Add the fruit shreds and the muslin bag of pips to the preserving pan with the water, bring to the boil then simmer over a medium to low heat for about 1½ hours, stirring from time to time, until the fruit is soft and the liquid has reduced by about half to about 1.2 litres.

Stir in the pineapple and cook for 15–20 minutes until softened, stirring from time to time but more frequently towards the end of cooking as the fruit mixture thickens. Squeeze the muslin bag of pips between two wooden spoons so that the juice drips back into the pan, then discard the bag.

Pour in the warmed sugar, stir well and cook over a low heat, stirring from time to time, until completely dissolved. Bring to the boil and boil rapidly for 15–20 minutes, stirring from time to time, until setting point is reached.

Take the pan off the heat and stir in the butter to disperse any remaining scum, if needed. Ladle the hot marmalade into warmed sterilised jars right to the top, then screw on lids or cover with waxed discs and cellophane tops secured with elastic bands. Leave to cool, then label and date. Store in a cool place.

VARIATION If you have some dark rum in the cupboard you might like to add 2 teaspoons to each warmed jar as you ladle in the warm marmalade. Stir well so that the rum flavour goes through the marmalade.

Tangerine and curaçao marmalade

Tangerines are lower in pectin than other citrus fruits. Boost this by adding fresh lemon juice and the squeezed lemon shells and pips.

700g (or about 8) tangerines, washed
and halved
3 lemons, washed and halved
1.2 litres water

1kg granulated sugar, warmed
15g unsalted butter (optional)
8 tsp orange curaçao, triple sec or
other orange liqueur

Squeeze the juice from the tangerines and lemons and reserve along with the lemon pips. Cut the tangerine peel and pith into fine shreds and add to a preserving pan.

Cut the lemon shells into chunks and tie in a square of muslin with any pips; add to the preserving pan with the water. Bring to the boil, cover and simmer over a medium to low heat for about 1 hour, stirring from time to time, until the tangerine shreds are softened.

Lift the muslin bag into a ladle and hold above the pan; using a wooden spoon, press the bag so that the juices run back into the pan. Discard the bag. You should have about 1 litre at this stage. Stir in the tangerine and lemon juice and the warmed sugar, and cook over a low heat, stirring from time to time, until completely dissolved. Bring to the boil and boil rapidly for 15–20 minutes until setting point is reached.

Take the pan off the heat and stir in the butter to disperse any scum, if needed. Add 2 teaspoons of orange liqueur to each warmed sterilised jar then ladle in the hot marmalade, stirring between ladlefuls so that the liqueur is evenly distributed. Fill jars right to the top, then screw on lids or cover with waxed discs and cellophane tops secured with elastic bands. Leave to cool, then label and date. Store in a cool place.

Lemon and ginger marmalade

This is lovely on toast or stirred through whipped cream to accompany a warm apple pie.

800g (about 8–9) lemons, washed and halved

1.5 litres water

85g root ginger, peeled and coarsely grated

1.4kg granulated sugar, warmed

15g unsalted butter (optional)

Squeeze the juice from the lemons and reserve along with the pips. Cut the lemon peel and pith into fine shreds and add to a large china or glass bowl. Tie the pips in muslin and add to the bowl with the water. Cover and leave at room temperature to soak for 4 hours or overnight. Pour the juice into a jug, cover and chill in the fridge.

The next day add the lemon shreds, muslin bag and water to a preserving pan and add the ginger. Bring to the boil, then simmer uncovered over a medium to low heat for 1¾–2 hours until the lemon shreds are very soft and the mixture has reduced down by almost half to about 1.2 litres. Squeeze the muslin bag between two wooden spoons so that the juice can drip back into the pan then discard the bag.

Pour in the reserved lemon juice and warmed sugar, stir together and cook over a low heat, stirring from time to time, until the sugar has completely dissolved. Bring to the boil and boil rapidly for 15–20 minutes, stirring from time to time, until setting point is reached.

Take the pan off the heat and stir in the butter to disperse any scum, if needed. Ladle into warmed sterilised jars right to the top, then screw on lids or cover with waxed discs and cellophane tops secured with elastic bands. Leave to cool, then label and date. Store in a cool place.

Index